FAITH OVER FEAR

HOW TO APPLY FAITH TO ANY
FEARFUL SITUATION.

JEREMY MCGARITY

WESTBOW
PRESS®
A DIVISION OF THOMAS NELSON
& ZONDERVAN

WestBow Press books may be ordered through booksellers or by contacting:

WestBow Press
A Division of Thomas Nelson & Zondervan
1663 Liberty Drive
Bloomington, IN 47403
www.westbowpress.com
844-714-3454

ISBN: 978-1-6642-7423-5 (sc)
ISBN: 978-1-6642-7424-2 (hc)
ISBN: 978-1-6642-7425-9 (e)

Library of Congress Control Number: 2022914091

Print information available on the last page.

WestBow Press rev. date: 09/30/2022

To the Skyline Church staff,

Thank you for walking through this season of coronavirus and lockdowns and mandates with such strong faith. When so many people were cowering in fear, you stood up and said, "We're going to walk in faith over fear."

I am honored to serve with such a faith-filled team!

CONTENTS

PREFACE

Faith, according to Hebrews 11:1 is "confidence in what we hope for and assurance about what we do not see" (NLT). And if you're reading this and you're a longtime Christian, or you grew up in the church, you've probably heard this definition before.

Or maybe you've picked up this book today, and you've walked away from the idea of the church and organized religion, but you've heard the word *faith*.

Or maybe you've picked up this book today, and you've never been to church and never known Jesus as anything more than a curse word or Jewish teacher or some guy Christians talk about all the time, but you've heard the word *faith*.

Regardless of where you come from or the ways in which you have or haven't experienced God, the definition Hebrews gives is a great definition, especially when everything in our lives is going well.

When we're healthy, when we're successful, when we're happy, and when our lives are free from struggle, pain, doubts, storms, or fear.

Fear comes into play when we anticipate or become aware of something dangerous that poses a threat to our well-being.[1] And in some ways, fear can be a really good thing. It's the built-in survival mechanism that keeps us from entering potentially life-threatening situations, and it helps us escape from places our bodies and minds believe to be dangerous.

But for Christians, fear can also be detrimental to the ways we experience and manifest faith if we let it linger unaddressed. If you don't profess to being a believer, fear can also be the thing holding you back from giving your life to Jesus.

If you're struggling to grow in your faith, this book is for you.

If you're struggling with doubts, this book is for you.

If you're staring down the eye of a storm, this book is for you.

If you're struggling with fear, this book is for you.

Friends, we were made for more than just wrestling and striving and struggling.

We were made for hope and connection and faith.

And I want to help you find it. Let's walk in faith over fear, together.

CHAPTER 1
WALKING IN FAITH OVER FEAR

You need to shut down the church! I couldn't believe what I was hearing. COVID was in full swing, and everything from governmental buildings and services to the local gym were closing. Now, concern was growing that any gathering could increase the spread of this unknown virus that was so deadly that the entire country of Italy was shut down with stay-at-home orders and travel lockdowns.

In the beginning of the pandemic, we wanted to make sure we helped people navigate this phenomenon. After gathering as much information as possible, we closed the church buildings but kept church going online. Over the course of the next several weeks, I did a deep dive into the science behind all these closures and soon realized it was fear, not scientific or statistical data, which was driving these closures.

After taking time to meet with our leadership teams and pray through what we were about to do, we knew there was only one way to respond to rampant fear in our community. It was time to live in *faith* over *fear*.

We opened Skyline Church to thousands of people who were so hungry for a sense of normalcy in their lives. Over the course of the next several weeks, we saw Skyline Church reach attendance numbers never experienced in the rich history of the church. We experienced more decisions for Christ, more baptisms, more people becoming members than ever before. We were witnessing a revival right in front of our eyes.

When we decided to walk in faith over fear, *everything* changed.

NUMBERS 13–14

Have you ever heard the expression about having nothing to fear but fear itself and wondered where it came from while thinking, "What kind of person isn't afraid of sharks?" Or spiders. Or heights. Or whatever it is that you're deathly afraid of.

Franklin Delano Roosevelt (affectionately known as FDR), the thirty-second president of the United States, used the phrase (that he paraphrased from Henry David Thoreau, an American transcendentalist writer) in his presidential inauguration speech some eight decades ago, right smack-dab in the middle of one of the largest and most devastating economic downturns in modern history: the Great Depression.[1]

Talk about having something to fear. Stock market crash. Massive unemployment.

The Dust Bowl.

How does humanity weather circumstances like these?

The Bible is chock-full of men and women who came up against difficult and sometimes even impossible circumstances and situations. We're talking giants of faith here: Moses, Esther, Abraham, David, and Paul, among many, many others.

Passing through the Red Sea with the Egyptian army on your heels, praying the walls of water hold?

Calling for an audience on behalf of your people with your husband-king when you know it's illegal to come before him without first being summoned?

Knowing you're the anointed king of Israel while your best friend's father hunts you down like an animal?

Being struck blind, imprisoned, shipwrecked, and finally martyred for a faith you initially persecuted?

How about crossing the Jordan into the long-awaited, long-anticipated Promised Land after four hundred years of Egyptian slavery?

I really love the book of Numbers. And not just because I'm a pastor. I love the book of Numbers because in between all the genealogies and numbered lists in this incredible book, there's some powerful wisdom. Like, really good wisdom about the effects of fear and faith as we live out the Christian life.

So, let me catch you up:

Moses has led the nation of Israel out of Egypt to freedom. They're heading toward the land that God has promised them.

Fun fact: God is always faithful to His promises (Joshua 21:45; 1 Kings 8:56; 2 Corinthians 1:20 NLT).

They've crossed the Red Sea with God holding the walls of water up only until His people are safely on the other side. Then he tears them down, drowning the Egyptian army that's right on their heels. They've been journeying through the desert for about two years when they come to the edge of the Jordan River. The children of Israel are about to cross over into the Promised Land at a place called Kadesh. They are literally standing on the periphery of the land that God had promised them during their four hundred years of slavery under Pharaoh, the land where they would have their own country, their own freedom.

When they get up to the edge of the water, just before they go in, Moses says to them, "I want twelve of you, one leader from each tribe, to go over and spy out this Promised Land. Bring back a report of what it's like."

So they go. They're gone for forty days and forty nights, and they come back with a mixed report.

Two of the leaders said, "This place is *awesome*. It's exactly how God told us it would be. Let's go. Right now" (Numbers 13:30 paraphrase).

Their names were Joshua and Caleb.

But the other ten said, "We can't go. Yes, it's beautiful and bountiful. But we can't do it. There are giants in the land, and there's a bunch of people who will kill us. No way we can take this land."

Anyone know their names? Anyone? (Bueller?)

Shaphat, Igal, Palti, Gaddiel, Ammiel, Sethur, Nahbi, Geuel, and Shammua (not the whale).

Here's the point:

Nobody remembers the negative guys. Nobody. But everybody remembers Joshua and Caleb.

Nobody names their kid after the negative guys. I don't know anyone named: Shaphat or Igal or Shammua. But I know a lot of Joshuas and Calebs.

Why?

Nobody remembers fearful people.

Nobody remembers the naysayers.

Nobody remembers the alarmists, the critics, the fear-mongers, the people who say it can't be done.

But the faithful and faith-filled? The people who say, in faith, "We're going to move forward?" We remember them.

But because those ten leaders chose fear over faith and because the entire generation of Israelites standing on the edge of the Jordan River, just a stone's throw away from the long-desired, painfully awaited Promised Land, chose to view their circumstances through fear over faith, they began grumbling and complaining and whining.

And God said, "Not one of them will set eyes on the land I so solemnly promised to their ancestors. No one who has treated me with such repeated contempt will see it" (Numbers 14:23 NLT).

Choosing fear over faith is always contemptible to God. He kept them out of the land He desired to give them and purposed for them because they refused to have eyes of faith.

And that is what we're going to explore here.

THROUGH EYES OF FEAR

So, what happens when we choose to view our difficult circumstances with eyes of fear?

We exaggerate our difficulties. We underestimate our abilities. We get discouraged. We complain. We eventually give up and blame God.

And Israel is no exception.

God has just done an amazing thing in delivering Israel from the most powerful nation in the world at the time, Egypt; from the most powerful leader of the day, Pharaoh; and from the world's most powerful army of charioteers and infantry.

He has just released them, miraculously gotten them out.

And just two years later, they've already forgotten all of that, worrying and fearful of some local tribe in the Promised Land.

How quickly we forget all the incredible things God has done for us. All the times He's gotten us out of trouble. All the times He's come through for us. All the times He's provided for us and taken care of us.

When we look at our problems with eyes of fear, our problems get bigger.

Remember that negative report from the ten leaders whose names we can't remember? They gave an account of the Promised Land in Numbers 13:27–29:

> We went to the land to which you sent us and, oh! It **does** flow with milk and honey! Just look at this fruit! The only thing is that the people

who live there are fierce, their cities are huge and well-fortified. Worse yet, we saw descendants of the giant Anak. Amalekites are spread out in the Negev; Hittites, Jebusites, and Amorites hold the hill country; and the Canaanites are established on the Mediterranean Sea and along the Jordan." (MSG, emphasis mine)

Now, the Anakim were of the tribe of Skywalker, and the force was strong with them.

Wait. That's another story. Back to Israel.

The next section, Numbers 13:31–33, says:

But the others said, "We can't attack those people; they're way stronger than we are." They spread scary rumors among the people of Israel. They said, "We scouted out the land from one end to the other—it's a land that swallows people whole. Everybody we saw was huge. Why, we even saw the Nephilim giants (the Anak giants come from the Nephilim). Alongside them we felt like grasshoppers. And they looked down on us as if we were grasshoppers." (MSG)

I want to point something out here.

The majority report is almost always fearful and negative. Anybody who's going to get something done in this world is going to have to go against the majority report—they're going to have to go against all the naysayers—because the majority of people in our world go through life with eyes of fear, not faith.

That's just our world.

They said, "It's a land that swallows people whole." The Hebrew word that's used here is *ākal*. Here's why it's important: It literally means "to be eaten up."[2]

These fearful spies came back to the people and said, "They're not only going to kill us; they're going to eat us. As a matter of fact, they're going to eat us alive! We can't do it."

Nobody wants to be eaten by cannibals. Naturally.

And despite the faith of Joshua and Caleb and the explicit promise of Israel's God, the people trusted the majority report.

Here's the problem: Negative, fearful attitudes are contagious.

When the Israelites walked up to the edge of the Jordan, they were excited. They were fired up. They were psyched that God was about to fulfill His promise to Israel.

Then the spies come back, wracked by fear, and give a terrifying report of the land.

And their fear spreads like a virus through the whole camp.

"We're going to get eaten!" "We're going to die!" "We can't go there!"

Suddenly, their fear of the tribes on the other side of the Jordan wasn't their only hang-up. As they allowed fear to creep in and take over, the people of Israel started underestimating their own God-given abilities.

The negative spies referred to themselves in Numbers 13:33 as grasshoppers.

Talk about low self-esteem. They're saying, "We're just insects to them. Little bugs. They're going to squash us."

Notice, they say, "Alongside them we felt like grasshoppers." That's their own self-image, and then it says, "And they looked down on us as if we were grasshoppers." How do they know what they looked like to the enemy? How could they know what the rival tribes in the Promised Land thought of them?

They assumed that, to the eyes of the enemy, the people of Israel were theirs for the taking.

There's a term for this. It's called fear projection. You tend to project your fears onto the people around you, and that's what Israel is doing here. They're projecting their fears.

Think about this: They've been slaves for four hundred years, and they've only been free a short time.

So, they have this fear of the unknown, of what's going to happen. They may be free of Egypt, but they're still mentally enslaved.

Now, let's just stop here for a minute.

This mental slavery is not a condition exclusive to Israel, or even to someone who's been physically enslaved. Mental shackles are present wherever and whenever we allow fear and the opinions of others to define us. You may have had somebody—a parent or a partner or a friend or a brother or a sister—say things about you, things that still wrap themselves around your mind because someone you cared about said you were worthless, that you wouldn't amount to anything. Or maybe they said something about your intelligence, your drive, your choices, your worth. And maybe you still carry those words with you, those ideas they had about who you are, as they play on loop in your head.

That is fear. A self-imposed prison of fear wherein you are enslaved to someone else's image of you.

You're not in Egypt anymore.

Don't underestimate your own abilities based on what someone said to you in your past.

Because when we do that, we get discouraged.

Numbers 14:1 says it like this: "The whole community was in an uproar, wailing all night long" (MSG).

They threw themselves a giant pity party, crying and weeping, "We're never going to get to the Promised Land! We can't do it! We can't do it!"

Wait a minute.

God had already promised to give them the land.

What's keeping them out? Their *fear*. When we're not living by faith, fear creeps in, and we get discouraged.

And when we have eyes of fear, we move from discouragement to griping, focusing on everything that's going to go wrong in our lives. In Numbers 14:2, after the all-night pity party, "All the people of Israel grumbled against Moses and Aaron. The entire community was in on it: "Why didn't we die in Egypt? Or in this wilderness?" (MSG).

First, they cry, and now they complain. They're being critical of their leaders. They're being critical of the situation.

This is an easy mentality to fall into when we face difficult situations.

And God doesn't want this for us. It goes back to our community, our *oikos*.

Are we patient in those situations? Are we grumbling? Are we complaining?

By the way, let me just say: highly critical people are always highly insecure people. It's a mentality dominated by fear. I'm going to criticize you to make me feel better about myself. In fact, I don't want *you* feeling good about *yourself* if *I'm* not feeling good about *myself.*

We underestimate our abilities, we get discouraged, we gripe about our lives, and then we eventually give up and blame God.

Notice what the Israelites say in Numbers 14:3: "Why has God brought us to this country to kill us? Our wives and children are about to become plunder. Why don't we just head back to Egypt? And right now!" (MSG).

Hold up.

God brought them there to give them the Promised Land. An incredible place. And instead of rejoicing over God's faithfulness, they blame him for their perceived inability to cross the Jordan. Yet, the reality is, God isn't the one holding them back. It's their fear. They're second guessing not only their own ability to take the land, something they're certain they can't do, but also God's purpose in even bringing them to this place. And in their fear, they're suddenly remembering the "good old days" of Egypt.

Excuse me?

Good old days? There were no "good old days" in Egypt. There were four hundred years of slavery. Why would they want to go back?

Let me offer a theory.

It was slavery, but it was safety. It was comfortable. They knew what to expect.

But on the other side of the Jordan River? Unknown. With our fears, at least we know what to expect.

A lot of people get stuck in "safe slavery." They're enslaved by a relationship, or a fear, or a habit, or a compulsion, or a thought, and they really don't like it, but they don't want to let go of it because at least it's predictable. It's comfortable.

I know what's in Egypt.

But the other side of the Jordan?

Some of you are doing that. Some of you are confusing slavery and safety. And they're not the same thing.

"I know it's a bad situation but at least it's predictable." "I know this habit is self-defeating but it's comfortable." "It's just who I am. It's what I do."

There is no real freedom without taking steps of faith to face the giants in your life.

Safety and freedom are on opposite ends of the spectrum. You're either moving toward safety and slavery, or you're moving toward faith and freedom. God made you a person of faith, a risk-taker. Don't die in the desert of your fears.

HOW DO WE DEFINE FAITH?

So, we've covered fear. What about faith?

What about Joshua and Caleb?

Before we go back to Kadesh and the banks of the Jordan, to the two spies whose faith affirmed God's promise to Israel, I think it would be helpful to define what we mean when we talk about faith in a biblical sense.

What is faith? It is the confident assurance that something we want is going to happen. It is the *certainty* that what we hope for is waiting for us, even though we cannot see it up ahead. (Hebrews 11:1 TLB, emphasis mine)

Think about that.

Faith is being certain of something that's going to happen, even though we can't see it right now. It has to do with your vision.

Faith, in its simplest form, is seeing life from God's perspective. Would you agree there's always more than one way of seeing things?

If you're married, you know that's true. If you have kids, you know that's true. Your husband or wife or children see things differently than you see them. But at the end of the day, it doesn't matter how I see things. And it doesn't matter how you see things.

What really matters is how God sees things. What is God seeing? What is His perspective?

We want to know how God sees things. And faith is learning how to see things from God's point of view.

Apostle Paul writes to the church at Ephesus in Ephesians 1:18: "I pray that your hearts will be flooded with light so that you can see something of the future he has called you to share" (NLT).

See, God wants to flood our hearts with light so that we can see the future that He has for us. And I can promise you this: That future is not full of fear. But it is filled with faith.

Romans 1:17 puts it this way: "This Good News tells us that God makes us ... right in (his) sight—when we put our faith and trust in Christ to save us. This is accomplished from *start to finish by faith*. As the Scripture says it, 'The (person) who finds life will find it through trusting God'" (TLB, emphasis mine).

Now I want to make a distinction here. Faith is not a feeling.

This is extremely important. Feelings are very unpredictable. You can't base your faith on how you feel. In fact, you need to understand that feelings often get in the way of faith because feelings are so unreliable and changeable, yet they're what we tend to rely on instead of our faith. We'll talk more in chapter 2 about how faith is tangible, but for now, let's just keep in mind that faith is not a feelings-based phenomenon.

Faith, in contrast to feelings, says, "I'm going to do the right thing because it's the right thing to do *regardless* of how I feel." It doesn't matter how I feel in the moment. What's most important is the choice to walk in faith because I know it's the right thing to do. Remember, faith is seeing life from God's perspective.

So, back to the Promised Land.

Joshua and Caleb came back with the ten other leader-spies having seen the same land and observed the same people. But instead of fearing the obstacles standing between Israel and the land flowing with milk and honey, the land promised to them by the God of Abraham, Joshua and Caleb returned with confidence that they could take it, and they spoke up *in faith*.

Let's pause for a moment.

Do you think Joshua and Caleb didn't feel fearful of going up against the tribes who were living on the other side of the Jordan? That they didn't feel the pressure of going against the majority report of the other leaders when speaking with Moses? That they were supernaturally equipped to only experience and express confidence and excitement at the prospect of war with neighboring tribes?

Maybe.

My guess is, they experienced some fear and some pressure. They were humans, too, after all. But the most notable difference between Joshua and Caleb and the other leaders was that those two didn't allow their feelings to dictate their faith, and it showed up in their response. This is going to be super important to the fate of Israel in a minute.

Back to Numbers.

Later, when the rest of Israel is griping and complaining and whining and doubting, and Moses is pleading for forgiveness on their behalf, God declares that the entire generation of Israel He's just rescued from slavery in Egypt and brought to the edge of the Jordan—within sight of this awesome place He's purposed for them—will not enter the land. They think life was better in Egypt? Not only do they forfeit the inheritance of the very God who's rescued them those countless times, but they get to wander and die in the wilderness instead.

Except for Joshua and Caleb. Why?

Because, as Hebrews 11:6 says: "Without faith it is impossible to please God, because anyone who comes to Him must believe that He exists and that He rewards those who earnestly seek Him" (NIV).

Did you know that God wants to reward you for having faith?

Listen, here's the reality: It's easy to seek God when the sun is shining, when the wind is at your back, and when everything is going great. But do we have faith in difficult times? When we're struggling, are we certain that God will come through? And do we express that confidence, allowing it to be seen? Because the reality is that your oikos, those people in your relational world, are always going to be watching.

And they want to know, *Christian*, does it work?

Does your faith have any bearing in difficult times?

Or is it only when things are going well that we talk about our faith?

The real test is in moments like these. The uncertainties of life. The challenges of life. The times when we're standing on the edge of something that could be exceptionally great, our own Promised Land, but we see the obstacles on the other side.

Do we react with fear, letting our emotions get the better of us and crowd out God's promises?

Or do we react with faith, acknowledging that God is both bigger and better than our feelings?

You see, until we understand how important it is to see everything in life through eyes of faith, we're not going to be growing as Christians, and we're not going to be able to live the life that God has called us to live unless we are walking, every single day, in faith. As a matter of fact, if we're not walking in faith, fear will paralyze us, just like it did that entire generation of Israelites.

And friends, wandering and dying in the wilderness doesn't sound too great to me.

THROUGH EYES OF FAITH

So, what does life look like when we see through eyes of faith? Fear exaggerates my problems.

Faith shrinks them. Every. Single. Time.

When you see your problem from God's point of view, everything becomes a lot more manageable.

Bottom line: If you have a big God, you have small problems. If you have a small god, you have big problems.

Genesis 18:14 asks: "Is anything too hard for the Lord?" (NLT). Was the Great Depression too hard for the Lord? No.

Is a global pandemic too hard for the Lord? No.

Is the Padres winning the World Series this year too hard for the Lord? Well...no.

In Matthew 19:26, Jesus said: "Humanly speaking, it is impossible. But with God everything is possible!" (NLT).

And *nothing* means not a single thing, folks. But it doesn't just stop there.

Faith also moves God to act on my behalf.

Now, don't get me wrong when I say this. I'm not talking about the health, wealth, and prosperity gospel that's out there that says everyone should be wealthy and healthy and if you're not, it's because you lack faith.

That's not what I'm talking about. That's a theology that sees God as a genie who works for us and serves us, not the other way around.

God is not your genie. God is God, and you're not. He is not there to cater to your every whim. He's just not.

But what I am talking about is what He very clearly says in His Word. In Matthew 9:29, Jesus said: "According to your *faith* let it be done to you" (NIV, emphasis mine).

What does that mean?

God says you get to choose how much He blesses your life (Matthew 9:29 NIV). Do you want to know how God moves and blesses people? It's not because we deserve it. It's not because someone is attractive, or born in a particular place, or is more intelligent than the next person. It's because of faith.

According to your *faith*, it will be done to you.

When we humbly, by faith, expect Him to act. Because God has made it clear that He wants to use you, bless you, and guide you.

According to your *faith*, it will be done to you.

Now look, if you expect God to do very little in your life, He'll probably do very little. If you expect God to do a lot in your life, He'll probably do a lot in your life. If you don't expect God to do anything, He won't do anything.

I've believed God for some really big things in my life, but it didn't start there. It started by developing the muscle of faith a little bit at a time. I'd believe God in the little things, and when He came through, I'd believe Him for something a little more, and He'd come through again. I just kept pressing and pushing and stretching and believing in faith, and God has done some really big things.

See, the problem with us is that we think the wrong thing moves God. But He's not moved by my complaints. God is never moved by my griping, my complaining, my grumbling, or my whining.

God is moved when I say, "God, I'm trusting you and I'm expecting you to keep your promise. You put your name on that promise, and I'm expecting you, *by faith*, to do it."

And when we live from a place of faith, we unlock the promises of God, which, by the way, number over seven thousand, according to scripture.

2 Corinthians 1:20 says: "For no matter how many promises God has made, they are all 'Yes' in Christ!" (NIV).

All the promises that God has made in His Bible, in His word, in His scripture, are in Christ.

But you must be a person of faith, a promise person. Let me put it this way:

You're out in the wilderness, hiking around, and you stumble across an old, broken-down cabin that's clearly unoccupied and dilapidated. Being the adventurous person that you are, you decide to check it out. Inside, you poke around through the dust and cobwebs, and you see a drawer. You find a letter in there that says: "To the person holding this note, you are entitled to one million dollars of my estate."

Now, that'd be pretty awesome. But it wouldn't do you any good if you didn't know the author—who he or she is and where to find him or her.

Same with the seven-thousand-plus promises of God. If you don't know the author, it doesn't do you any good. You've got to know the Author to claim the promises.

The promises of the Bible only apply to those who know the author, to those who know the name of Jesus.

And hear me, all the promises of God are "Yes" in Christ. When you know him personally, it unlocks the vast array of promises that

God has for you, including the 365 times it says in the Word of God, "Do not fear."

That's one for every day.

And it's through that faith, that God-perspective, that we're able to find strength in difficulties.

Think of Joshua and Caleb, staring down adversaries in the Promised Land and going against the majority report of the fear-stricken leaders because they know God is capable, but the people just won't listen. Talk about a difficult situation.

It's like that quote: "A smooth sea never made a skilled sailor." (Also, FDR. Who knew?) It's in the rough seas that a sailor learns to sail, not in the calm and uneventful waters near the shoreline.

It's the same thing in our Christian walk.

Why is this one important? Because faith doesn't always take you out of the problem.

The promise of God is that faith is going to get you *through* the problem.

We will always have troubles and difficulties in life on this side of heaven. And faith doesn't take us out of the storm. But it does give us the ability to handle it. Jesus spoke in John 16:33: "In this world you will have trouble, but take heart, for I have overcome the world" (NIV).

Faith produces persistence. It gives you the ability to bounce back. Study after study has shown that the most important characteristic you could teach a child and probably the most important characteristic you need in your own life if you're going to walk strongly in faith is resilience. It's the ability to bounce back, to keep going. Nobody goes through life with an unbroken chain of successes. Everybody has failures, flops, duds, and mistakes. We all embarrass ourselves. We all have pains. We all have problems. We all have pressures.

Paul writes in 2 Corinthians 4:8–9: "We are pushed hard from all sides. But we are not beaten down. We are bewildered. But that doesn't make us lose hope. Others make us suffer. But God does not desert us. We are knocked down. But we are not knocked out" (NIV).

Where do you get resilience like that? Our favorite five-letter word. Faith.

The space race in the '60s between the Americans and the Russians was all about who could get to the moon first. And for a while, Russia was ahead. They sent up the first man to circle the earth. His name was Yuri Gagarin.[3]

Now, Gagarin was a very famous Russian cosmonaut and, notably, an atheist. When he came down, he said, "You know, I was up there, and I was an eagle. I could see the heavens, everything." Then he said, "I searched the heavens, and I found no God. I looked for God in the heavens when I was up there and I did not see him, so there is no God."

A few months later, John Glenn (who, by the way, was a man of faith), an astronaut in the Gemini Program,[4] went up and circled the earth three times. When Glenn came down, he exclaimed, "I saw God everywhere. I felt his glory in the heavens. I saw his presence in the stars, I felt his power in the sun. I saw God everywhere."

Which one was telling the truth? They both were.

Jesus said in John 3:3: "I tell you the truth, unless you are born again, you cannot see the Kingdom of God" (NLT).

You can't see what God is doing behind the scenes.

You can't see the miracles.

You can't see that He's going to bring good out of the bad situations of life on this side of heaven if you don't have faith.

A very important promise I want to close this chapter with is from Philippians 4:6–7: "Do not be anxious about anything, but in every situation, by prayer and petition, with thanksgiving, present your requests to God. And the peace of God, which transcends all understanding, will guard your hearts and your minds in Christ Jesus" (NIV).

Have faith, friends.

CHAPTER 1 STUDY QUESTIONS

Question: What are some of your biggest fears? Take a moment to list a few of them. How is God sovereign over those fears? In what ways does God make His presence known to you when you encounter those fears? What happens to those fears when God draws near?

_____

_____

_____

_____

_____

_____

Question: The Bible tells us that faith is something unseen but very tangible and that it isn't solely an emotional experience. How does the biblical definition of faith impact your understanding of who God is? How do you experience faith?

_____

_____

_____

_____

_____

_____

Journal: Recall a situation in which you experienced fear. How did you respond? Numbers 13–14 provides a powerful example of what happens when we place our trust in God's power, promises, and presence, especially in situations that feel impossible. How is your response like or different from the spies that the Israelites sent across the Jordan? How would your own experience of fear be different if you responded in faith instead of fear?

_____

_____

_____

_____

_____

_____

Action: Read through Hebrews 11, commonly known as the "Hall of Faith." What did each of the people mentioned in the chapter have in common (besides faith in God)? How did their faith inform the way they lived their lives?

_____

_____

_____

_____

_____

_____

CHAPTER 2
INCREASING YOUR FAITH

Mark 6:34–44 relates one of the most famous miracles of Jesus Christ. In fact, it's so famous that it's the only miracle recorded four times in the Bible. It's found in all four of the gospels: Matthew, Mark, Luke, and John. And it was the most famous, widely known, widely witnessed miracle of Jesus's ministry.

It's commonly called the miracle of feeding the five thousand, though far more than five thousand were there. In the historical context, that number would've only included the men who were present, but aside from an army, wherever you have five thousand men, you probably have five thousand women and likely at least ten thousand children.

So, we probably have somewhere between fifteen thousand and twenty thousand men, women, and children gathered on a remote hillside near Galilee under a sweltering sun where they have been for hours, listening to Jesus teach. And they're getting hungry.

Jesus's disciples come to Him, express their concerns about the lack of food and the abundance of people and urge Jesus to send the crowd away to take care of their own hunger. Reasonable response to the problem at hand, right? And they probably expect Jesus to do what they're asking and send the crowds away.

But Jesus doesn't do that.

Instead, he challenges His disciples to see to the people's needs. By extension, He's asking them to embrace faith in Him over their fear of failure. And to the disciples, this is an outrageous task. They exclaim in Mark 6:37 that to feed the whole crowd "would take more than half a year's wages!" (NIV)—a daunting figure no matter how you look at it, not to mention the logistics of transporting and distributing the food to this massive crowd.

But instead of starting from scratch, Jesus asks, "How many loaves do you have?" (Mark 6:38 NIV). His disciples find a boy who'd brought along with him what amounted to a sack lunch— five loaves of bread, which in those days would've been more like small barley squares (these would be similar in size to mini-muffins today), and two fish, likely the size of sardines—and reported back to Jesus.

This is an insurmountable task, right? No way this measly offering of muffins and sardines was going to satiate a crowd of upward of twenty thousand people.

But wouldn't it be miraculous if it did?

Jesus never did a miracle to show off. But He always did perform miracles to teach principles of faith and to reveal who God is and what He's like. And here, as Jesus blesses the bread and fish and begins breaking off pieces, and the pieces multiply until they're distributed to the outer stretches of the crowd (Mark 6:41–42 NLT), we see what He can do with the little we have to offer and how He gives us ways to *increase our faith*.

HOW TO GROW YOUR FAITH

This miracle story begs the question: What do you do when you need to increase your faith?

There are times—generally, but not always—when life is going well, and we're feeling strong in our faith but know we can still increase it, and those times are awesome. We love those times.

But there are also times when we feel a lack of faith, and we need to increase it. In uncertain and difficult times, it's easy for our faith to waver. Yet, it's in these uncertainties and difficulties that God wants to grow our faith. The cool thing about those circumstances is that the more impossible a situation seems, the more we get to see God come through.

It's important to note here that faith is not abstract. We often tend to think of faith as ethereal; it's out there, but we don't physically engage with it. But faith is tangible. It's very touchable, very seeable, very feelable (we are 100 percent coining that phrase). There's an experience of faith that you don't just know, but that you can also feel, see, and even touch.

And that experience starts with paying attention to our own needs and to the needs around us.

When we're in need of more faith, we need to recognize and acknowledge our own need. And this can be a hard task, friends.

We don't like to admit our problems. We like to hide them, cover them up, blame other people, and pretend our problems don't exist.

Anything to keep our pride intact.

But the first principle of this story is recognizing our need for God to intervene. He doesn't save us until we see a need to be saved. Jesus says in Matthew 7:7: "Ask and it shall be given to you" (NIV). And this admonition isn't unique to Jesus's teaching. Over twenty times in the New Testament, we're commanded to ask.

But it doesn't stop there. We also need to be aware of the needs of others. This is what we see in the disciples' response to Jesus telling them to feed the people.

Man, this is what I love about the disciples. They're just like you and me. They're not superheroes. They're just people trying to follow

Jesus, but they do it so imperfectly. They put blinders on that kept them from seeing and engaging with the needs of the crowd on that sweltering afternoon.

HERE'S WHY WE DON'T PAY ATTENTION TO NEEDS

Their first mistake? Procrastinating.

Anybody could have figured out that these people were going to get hungry sometime. They're out in the middle of the desert. There's no place to eat, no Chick-Fil-A, no In-N-Out, no McDonald's, and the disciples should've been able to anticipate that a crowd of this size—and really of any size—was going to get hungry, sooner rather than later.

And they procrastinated, choosing instead to ignore the problem, maybe in hopes that the crowd would disperse and take care of their own needs and absolve the disciples of the task and responsibility of feeding them. And we do this with a lot of our problems as well. We tend to ignore the problem and hope it goes away.

We delay, procrastinate, pretend it doesn't exist, and look the other way.

But the truth is, procrastination only makes a problem worse.

And where there's procrastination, excuses are sure to follow. Notice what the disciples say: "Send the people away" (Mark 6:36 NIV). Instead of pressing in and welcoming the needs of the crowd, the disciples wanted the people out of sight and out of mind. If they didn't have to witness the needs of the crowd, they wouldn't have to do anything to meet their needs. Instead of taking responsibility for the people's hunger, they shift responsibility, essentially saying, "Jesus, we didn't ask these people to come see You. It's not our fault that they're here and that they didn't bring any food with them. So, it's not our responsibility to feed them. They're hungry? Tell them to get lost!"

How many times has this mentality been true of our own lives? How often have we shifted the responsibility to others and made excuses for why we couldn't, wouldn't, or shouldn't have met the needs we've witnessed in the people and the communities around us?

But instead of letting the disciples sweep the needs of this massive crowd of anxious onlookers under the rug, Jesus responds with compassion, and instead of telling them to go away, Jesus tells the disciples to feed them!

He desires to meet their physical needs, knowing that He can't address their spiritual needs if they're not willing to listen.

See, preachers worth their salt know that when people are hungry and tired, they aren't listening.

Just like the disciples on this crowded, hungry hillside, we have a very human tendency to make excuses for those moments when we choose to ignore situations that will grow our faith. We want to pass on the responsibility of caring for others, for repenting of sin, for seeking reconciliation. We want to say, "It's not my fault. It's society's fault. It's the environment's fault. It's the asphalt." We blame other things for the way we choose to respond—or not.

But with Jesus, it doesn't matter how we got into the situation we find ourselves in. What matters is how we react and respond to our circumstances.

We see in this account in Mark that making excuses and passing off responsibility is not the attitude God calls us to in overwhelming situations. Instead, this account challenges us to assess whether we have a servant's heart, a heart that says,

"Yeah, let's feed these people," or

"How can I make a difference here?" or

"How can I love this person as God has called me to?"

But Mark's account makes it abundantly clear that we can have results or excuses, but we can't have both.

Excuses naturally flow from inconvenience, and the response of Jesus's disciples after He tells them to take care of the crowd is no exception. When He asks them to feed this crowd of fifteen thousand to twenty thousand people—a massive, daunting task even by today's standards—but can you imagine having to do this just before the first century with no modern conveniences for transport or food storage? Yikes! They argue with him, saying, "That would take more than half a year's wages! Are we to spend that much on bread and give it to them to eat?" (Mark 6:37 NIV).

A task like this is wildly inconvenient, and the disciples would much rather have the crowd take the initiative and feed themselves. They argue not only the logistical inconvenience—gathering the food, bringing it back to the hillside, and distributing it—but they argue against the sheer expense of providing sufficient food for a crowd of this size.

And the disciples let their fear overcome their faith.

Most of the disciples wouldn't have been wealthy men—Andrew, Peter, James, and John were fishermen (Matthew 4:18–22), while Matthew was a tax collector (Matthew 10:3) and likely the only one with any real wealth to contribute to Jesus's ministry. Even so, it would be an enormous expense to buy food to satiate the hunger of such a large crowd.

Taking everything into consideration, this seems like an insurmountable thing that Jesus is asking of them.

What they had forgotten was who was there with them—Jesus Christ, the Son of God—standing next to them, scanning the hungry, sunburned faces of the crowd. This is the guy who can turn stones to bread and who had legions of angels at his beck and call. The King of the universe is standing right there with them, and they're trying to figure out how this could even be possible without a Costco anywhere nearby!

Let's be honest; we do the same thing.

We know there's something big out there that we need to do, and we find all the reasons why:

Why we can't get involved.

Why it's not our fault or our responsibility.

Why the logistics won't work.

Why the task is too insurmountable.

But the same God who stood there, sweating on that hillside among the disciples and the crowd, stands with us, especially in those tasks that He's called us to do.

WALKING IN FAITH

According to Romans 8:31: "If God is for us, who can ever be against us?" (NLT). By faith we can step into those tasks, trusting that we are not alone in them, knowing that God equips us because He's both ready and willing to use what we already have to offer.

Instead of asking the disciples to start from scratch, Jesus asks them what they have to work with, and they report back, "Five small loaves of bread and two fish" (Mark 6:38 NLT). We've got to wonder why He did this. He's God. The same God who provided manna during Israel's years in the wilderness after He leads them out of slavery in Egypt (Exodus 16). He could've done this again, which would've required no legwork from the disciples. And it would've been miraculous. But what good would it have done for the tangible expression of the disciples' faith?

It would've been so easy for Jesus to solve the problem for them, right then and there.

No mess.

No hassle.

No challenge.

But that's the clincher.

God desires our obedience because obedience is one of the chief tangible ways in which we demonstrate our love for and faith in God.

And it's difficult to be obedient without faith because God often calls us to obedience with crazy difficult things.

For instance, feeding a crowd of fifteen thousand to twenty thousand people camped out on a hillside in a remote area near the Sea of Galilee. If we aren't challenged by the way God calls us to respond to our circumstances, there is no room for our faith to grow.

When you need to see your faith increase, God always starts with what we already have—faith and resources alike. It's like when you're starting a home improvement project. You wouldn't march straight on to your (first and almost inevitably of many) Home Depot trips without first evaluating what you already have at home. You'd start by evaluating what you have to work with and ask yourself, "What have I got, and how am I using it?" It's the same concept with faith. You take the energy, the time, the money, the relationships, the talent, or whatever it is that you have, and you give it to God, who will take what you have and use it for His kingdom purposes—even when the circumstances you find yourself called to feel impossible. Not only does He take what you have, but He increases it for His good purposes!

And God loves to ask His children to do the impossible because He wants to increase our faith. In fact, all four gospel writers recount this miracle, including John who writes, "He asked this only to test [them], for He already had in mind what he was going to do" (John 6:6 NIV).

Jesus wasn't sweating this problem. He'd seen the need long before His disciples did, and He had a plan in place. Like gold refined by fire, He wants to test our faith (1 Peter 1:7), not as a stumbling block but as a means of growing our faith and trust in Him. It's through trials and big asks that He demonstrates His character, His trustworthiness, and His constancy in coming through for us in every moment from the mundane to the miraculous.

We see numerous instances of this trial by fire throughout the Bible, Old and New Testament alike (Joseph being sold into slavery by his brothers, Esther in King Xerxes's court, Daniel in the lions' den). If we're faithful, faith-filled, and obedient in these moments of testing, great blessings follow (Joseph's stewardship of Egyptian wealth, Esther saving the Jews in Persia, Daniel's survival).

Sometimes we get to see the miracle; sometimes we get to be the miracle, and sometimes we get to receive the miracle.

When we are attentive to the needs around us and are willing to use what we have to work with—the little talent, the little ability, the little money, the little time, or in this case, the little basket of loaves and fish—and we surrender that to Jesus, He not only increases what we've offered, but he increases our faith in the process.

In John's account of the feeding of the five thousand, he writes that Andrew, one of the disciples, found a little boy in the crowd who'd brought a sack lunch (John 6:8–9 NLT). It wasn't much, just five barley loaves that were essentially muffins and a couple of fish, likely dried sardines. I'm sure that in that crowd of fifteen thousand to twenty thousand people, somebody else had brought a bigger and better meal, but Andrew found this little boy with a pocketful of muffins and sardines to bring to Jesus.

I wish the Bible followed the story of this little boy because I'm willing to bet on the blessings that followed him. This little boy became the hero not because he had the biggest meal or the best meal but because he gave what he had to Jesus in faith.

And Jesus used it.

Mark 6:41 describes that "Jesus took the five loaves and the two fish. He blessed the food and broke the loaves and He kept giving them to the disciples to set before the people" (NASB).

This is interesting. I don't know how He did it but evidently as He broke the bread, it just kept multiplying. He'd break off a piece, and there was another piece in its place. And this massive crowd bore witness to this continual breaking and rebreaking of bread and fish that never seemed to run out. It was miraculous, and that's why it's recorded four times by four authors. Significantly, this miracle illustrates that God will use whatever I give Him because God likes to use ordinary people to accomplish extraordinary tasks.

Notice the kind of giving that this little boy had that sparked a miracle.

He gave it willingly, cheerfully, and immediately.

There was no grudge or complaint or resentment or worry from this boy.

There was no hesitation on his part, no frantic inner monologue about what he was going to eat now that he'd given his lunch to this Jewish teacher that everyone was curious about.

In fact, his attitude wasn't unlike that of the disciples when Jesus called them to follow, and they dropped everything and came to Him immediately. Neither the disciples nor this little boy could possibly know what God was going to do with what they'd given Him. But because they'd given Him everything and given everything to Him willingly, cheerfully, and immediately, God blessed them.

God does not desire our sacrifices, but He does desire our hearts, and when we give of ourselves—our time and our resources—we demonstrate a willing faith and obedience to God. He wants our lives and our hearts more than our tithes and giving simply for the sake of giving. And this concept is also why the Bible says in Matthew 6:21: "For where your treasure is, there your heart will be also" (NIV).

Let me tell you what God does when you give faithfully.

In Luke 6:38 he writes: "Give, and you will receive. Your gift will return to you in full—pressed down, shaken together to make room for more, running over, and poured into your lap" (NLT).

God provides us opportunities to give to test our trust and to grow our faith. Here's the truth: The more generous you are with your money, your time, your energy, your service, and your encouragement, the more God is going to bless and move and work in you.

When you give, you can trust Jesus to increase what you've given back to Him. I trust Jesus to increase whatever I give Him. It may not be much (just muffins and sardines) but notice what happened in Mark 6:42–43: "Everyone ate and had enough. Then the disciples took up twelve baskets full of what was left of the bread and the fish" (GNB).

Everyone ate and was satisfied, and there was still more. Above and beyond.

Can I ask you something? What do you not have enough of in your life?

If you're lacking in provision in your life, it means you're not giving what you have to God.

If you lack money, you're not giving your first portion to God.

If you're lacking in your relationships, you're not giving that area of your life to God.

It's so important for our faith to commit to putting Jesus first and giving Him what He's already entrusted to us. Whatever you give completely to God, He increases and blesses it in return.

The gospel writers make it clear. Everyone ate and had enough. Can you imagine that kid going home with twelve baskets full of leftovers? Can you imagine the look on his mom's face when she sent her son out with five muffins and two sardines, and he comes home with baskets and baskets full of food? It's an incredible thing—God always provides when we walk in faith. There's a great passage in 2 Corinthians 9:6–8 that says:

"Remember this: Whoever sows sparingly will also reap sparingly, and whoever sows generously will also reap generously. Each of you should give what you have decided in your heart to give, not reluctantly or under compulsion, for God loves a cheerful giver. And God can bless you abundantly, so that in all things, at all times, having all that you need, you will abound in every good work" (NIV).

If you give away criticism, you're going to get back criticism, but exponentially.

If you give away encouragement, you're going to get back encouragement.

If you give away your time to help others, you're going to find you have more time than you would have had if you'd saved it for yourself.

Scripture makes it clear that we reap what we sow because God wants to teach us to become givers.

Of mercy, of time, of money, of encouragement, of peace, of love.

The chief desire and purpose of the Christian life is to become more like our Creator, and we can't do that if we're clinging with tight fists to the things—whatever they may be—that He's given us to steward with a heart rooted in Him.

And a heart rooted firmly in God, in faith, is a generous one. John 3:16 expresses the generosity of God, who loved this world, loved us so much that He was willing to give up His beloved Son to make a way for us to come to Him and experience His love in all its depth and richness and fullness. And until we learn and embrace this principle, we can't experience a tangible faith in the reality of our everyday lives.

God loves to do miracles through people, whether through His reluctant disciples or the eager little boy with a lightly laden lunchbox. He could have provided food for the crowd in any number of ways, but He chose instead to work through His people so that we would know Him—His character, His love, His provision—in ever-new ways. What we often wait for God to do for us, God is waiting to do through us.

CHAPTER 2 STUDY QUESTIONS

Question: Reflect on your relationship with God. How would you describe your faith—its amount, its expression, and its strength?

_____

_____

_____

_____

_____

_____

Question: Recall a time when you recognized someone else's needs. How did you respond? Did you try to meet those needs? If not, what held you back?

_____

_____

_____

_____

_____

_____

Journal: Make a list of the gifts and resources God has blessed your life with. How are you using those gifts and resources? Think about the ways in which you can use what God has given you to bless and take care of others.

_____

_____

_____

_____

_____

_____

Action: Think about the people in your oikos, your relational network (i.e., family, friends, church community). What needs do you see? How can you meet those needs this week?

_____

_____

_____

_____

_____

_____

CHAPTER 3
JESUS CALMS THE STORM

MARK 4:36–41.

There's something about storms for many people that creates a sinking, depressing feeling. We've all had our share of storms.

There are various types of storms in life, right?

I mean, we have situational storms, like the COVID-19 pandemic, with things that crop up in our lives that we have no control over—suddenly, they're just *there*. And we must learn how to deal with it.

Then there are relational storms. Things just aren't going well with your spouse, your kids, your neighbor, your coworker.

These might be longer and more drawn out. They're the kind of storm you learn to weather over the long haul.

And then there's emotional storms where we can be engaged in an inner war of emotions. These are sometimes called secret storms because we tend to keep these things pent up inside. Maybe we're consumed with worry or jealousy or overcome by guilt or raging with anger or paralyzed by fear.

Here's the thing about storms: They rob us of peace.

Jesus said something very important in John 14:27: "I am leaving you with a gift—peace of mind and heart. And the peace I give is a gift the world cannot give. So, don't be troubled or afraid" (NLT).

I love that.

The Bible says three things about the storms of life that I want you to get.

Storms in life are inevitable—unavoidable, even.

Storms in life are unpredictable. They come suddenly and unexpectedly, and we don't get a warning.

Storms in life are impartial. They don't play favorites, and they're not discerning.

Let's unpack this a little.

THE INEVITABILITY OF STORMS

The language of the Bible is intentional and good for instruction, always. And the word choice that James uses in James 1:2 is a perfect example. He writes, "*When* troubles of any kind come your way…" (NLT, emphasis mine).

This is a significant distinction, friends.

Notice how he doesn't say, "*If* you face trials." These trials James talks about are inevitable for those of us living out the Christian life. They're not a hypothetical event; they're intrinsic to the Christian life—a guarantee, if you will. In fact, you can count on it! You will face storms in life.

Nobody goes through life sailing smoothly from the cradle to the grave. We'll all experience tough times.

You're either coming out of a storm, you're in the middle of one, or you're heading toward one.

I know what you're thinking—super uplifting.

This is the reality of life here on earth, but bear with me.

THE UNPREDICTABILITY OF STORMS

In Mark's gospel account, we encounter a literal storm, one that shakes up even seasoned fishermen. We'll get into it in more depth later in the chapter, but I want to draw our attention to another aspect of the nature of storms.

Mark writes, "But soon a fierce storm came up. High waves were breaking into the boat, and it began to fill with water" (4:37 NLT).

We'll explore the cultural and historical context of this storm in a bit, but for now, remember that many of the disciples were fishermen who had been out on the Sea of Galilee numerous times. They would've known the currents and weather patterns, and yet they weren't able to predict this storm, let alone its ferocity. And I believe that this raises an important point.

We may be knowledgeable, discerning, intelligent, and thoughtful people. We may be careful and cautious. We may be intentional and purposeful.

But try as we may, we cannot predict the things that will happen to us—those proverbial "storms" that catch us off guard.

THE IMPARTIALITY OF STORMS

The third aspect of storms is a tough one.

And I don't mean tough to understand, but a difficult one to accept.

Storms are not discerning. Storms are impartial.

They happen to good people, and they happen to bad people. They happen to believers, and they happen to unbelievers.

Scripture is clear. Matthew 5:45 says it like this: "He sends rain on the just and the unjust" (NIV).

You see, being a Christian does not exempt us from getting caught in and experiencing the storms of life. A misconception in Christianity is that the only time believers experience storms is when they're disobeying God.

That is not true, friends.

When you're going through a tough time, don't automatically assume that you must be outside of God's will. You may be exactly where God wants you to be. Right in the middle of the storm.

The disciples were caught in that storm because they *obeyed* God.

In Mark 4:35 (MSG), Jesus said, "Let's go across to the other side," and the disciples climbed into the boat and set out for the other shore.

They were obeying God; they were in the center of His will, and yet they were sailing right into a storm.

The fact is that God has not promised us a storm-free life. This is not heaven where everything is perfect and where God's will is perfectly done. This is earth, where things aren't done perfectly, where we struggle with sickness, with difficult coworkers, with family relationships, with mental health, and with sin.

And this side of heaven has the potential for some pretty intense storms.

So, if storms are inevitable, unpredictable, and impartial, then the questions we really need to ask ourselves are:

What is my response going to be? How am I going to respond to the storms that are inevitably, unpredictably, and impartially going to happen in my life?

There are two ways we can respond to storms. And they're both evident in this story in the way the disciples responded versus the way that Jesus responded. And the way they responded emphasizes the differences between doubt and fear and faith.

When we face storms in life, we have a couple of options:

We can be filled with panic.

And this is the response the disciples chose.

Mark 4:38b asks: "Teacher, don't you care if we drown?" (NIV).

Why are they asking Him this? Doesn't Jesus know what's going on?

I'd wager that He did, being fully God and fully man, know what was happening. But the disciples, some of whom hadn't come to realize Jesus's divinity in full yet, are concerned because while they're bailing water out of a rapidly flooding deck, Jesus is asleep, undisturbed and unconcerned, below (Mark 4:37–38 NIV).

Now, keep in mind, these guys were not novices. Many of these men had been fishermen by trade. They'd been out on the Sea of Galilee lots of times. They know what a bad storm is—what it looks like, what it feels like, when it was time to throw in the towel (or net, if you will), and return to shore.

But this one was different. Life-threatening, even. So much so, that these seasoned fishermen felt like they had to convince Jesus that now was not a great time for a nap.

Now, something you must understand about the Sea of Galilee is that its topography lends itself well to creating insanely dangerous storms that crop up extremely quickly.

Notably, Mount Hermon sits to the north of the Sea of Galilee with mountain ridges flanking either side to create a perfect wind tunnel. Something about the shape and the wind currents make it a fantastic spot for a sudden and deadly storm. This is known as a squall.[1]

The disciples would've been able to recognize when a squall was coming. And they knew that this wasn't something to be taken lightly. In fact, many people had lost their lives after getting stuck in storms like this. It's entirely possible—likely, even—that the fishermen among Jesus's followers had personally known people lost in squalls on the Sea of Galilee.

Naturally, the disciples are nervous and likely thinking that Jesus doesn't understand the danger they're in—after all, He's just a carpenter, no wonder He's still sleeping. How would He know about the dire implications of the squall they've found themselves caught in?

They panicked. And that's our typical reaction when a storm comes. We, like the disciples, react in fear instead of responding in faith. We wonder if Jesus even notices the storm we're dealing with, and if He does notice, we wonder if He cares.

Does Jesus care that I'm drowning in debt?

Does Jesus care that I'm dealing with infidelity?

Does Jesus care that I'm struggling with depression?

We tend to fall into this mind-set because so often we think that it's God's priority to make our lives safe and comfortable.

But God's goal is to grow us and to glorify Himself through the experiences of our lives. And we do that by walking in faith over fear.

Through storms.

Through difficulties.

Through the coronaviruses of life so that nonbelievers would see God at work through believers.

You see, storms are a testament to the work and sovereignty and loving watch-care of our God. He calls us to be good witnesses, regardless of our circumstances (good thing we've got Jesus in our boat, huh?)

So, there is an alternative to being filled with panic.

We can be filled with peace.

And where the disciples responded with panic, Jesus responded to the squall—the storm—with peace.

In verse 38, Mark writes, "Jesus was in the stern, sleeping on a cushion" (NLT).

The storm is raging. Thunder is pounding, lightning is striking, waves are crashing relentlessly against the boat that's being thrown around in the Sea of Galilee like a rag doll. Water is everywhere. There isn't a surface on this vessel that isn't soaked through. The disciples are bailing water out like their life depends on it (because it does). And Jesus?

He's asleep.

Something notable about this story, this passage, is that it demonstrates the humanity of Jesus. He'd been teaching and preaching and healing people all day, and He was exhausted.

If you ever wonder, "Can Jesus really relate to what it's like to be human, to how tired I feel?" He absolutely can.

But more than that, I believe that this is a picture of what it looks like to have complete trust in God. Jesus was not worried by the storm at all. He was setting an example for the disciples.

Let me ask you something: Did Jesus know there was going to be a storm before He even got into the boat?

Without a doubt. He knew they were sailing right into a storm. But instead of grounding the boat or waiting out the storm, Mark's account says he grabbed a cushion, laid down, and took a nap. And in the process, He taught His disciples about faith.

Nothing ever surprises God. Ever.

It's ironic to me that Jesus is sleeping in the storm because one of the telltale signs that we're experiencing a storm is that we start *losing* sleep.

When we're in the middle of a storm, we lay awake at night, tossing and turning, going over and over it in our mind, trying to figure it out, worrying, and incessantly asking, "*What if...*"

Did you know the sleep aid industry in America is a $70 billion dollar?[2] That's billion with a "b," folks. Ours is a culture that focuses on worry, and our sleep reflects that.

But Jesus?

Jesus can go to sleep anywhere and in the middle of anything. Including a sudden and deadly squall on the Sea of Galilee.

We have choices when we're facing a storm.

We can either take one from the disciples' book and panic, or we can imitate Jesus's profound trust in the Father and be at peace in those situational, relational, and emotional storms.

The fact is that sometimes sleeping can be a statement of faith.

Think about this: Sometimes the circumstances and situations going on in our lives are simply too big.

When we turn problems over and over in our minds, problems that we know are too big for us to solve and too far outside of our control, we reach a point where the only (and best) course of action is to give it to God and go to sleep. And that's a statement of faith. Sleeping. Who knew?

Evidently, Jesus did.

So, let's say we want to imitate Jesus and choose to trust Him in our storms instead of panicking.

Where do you get that kind of peace in a storm?

We remember God's presence.

He's with us. He's right there in the boat with us—sinking or sailing.

The disciples had seen Jesus perform miracle after miracle, and now this same man who had fed the five thousand and healed the sick and restored the lame and proven His God-ness to them repeatedly was in their boat—and yet they still worried.

If we're in a storm, this first thing we must remember is that God is always with us.

There will never be anything you must face in this life alone. Never.

God has promised every believer, "I am with you always" (Matthew 28:20 NIV) and "I will never leave you nor forsake you" (Hebrews 13:5 NKJV).

The prophet Isaiah writes in 43:1–2: "Do not be afraid ... When you go through deep waters, I will be with you. When you go through rivers of difficulty, you will not drown" (NLT).

You don't need to worry if Jesus is in your boat— even if He's resting. Which is, evidently, also what we're called to do if we're to experience peace amid storms.

WE REST IN GOD'S CARE

God cares about what we go through.

If it helps, repeat this over and over until you get it in your mind. How much does He care? Infinitely. Read the Bible. Read the seven thousand promises in this book about His care for you. Speak this truth over your life daily, and God will be faithful to meet you in it.

The more you read and understand and rest in scripture, the more you will understand His care for you.

First Peter 5:7 says it like this: "Cast *all* your anxiety on Him because He cares for you" (NIV, emphasis mine).

The more we go to God, the more peace we have in this life.

It's easy to skip surrender. We worry about all kinds of things, and some are reasonable while others aren't. But Peter doesn't encourage us to only bring the big, substantiated, and valid worries to God. Instead, we're encouraged to bring *all* our worries to Him.

That's the one thing that the disciples did right in our passage. When they became fearful, they took their fear to Jesus. And they didn't hold back. Because they knew, despite their panic and fear, that He was the only one who could do anything about it.

And it is from this place of surrender that we, amid storms, rely on God's control.

Let His power see you through.

Mark 4:39 says: "Jesus got up, rebuked the wind and said to the waves, 'Quiet! Be still.' Then the wind died down and it was completely calm" (NIV).

There's two parts to the miracle in this story. First, Jesus got the storm to stop.

Miraculous, no doubt.

But then there's a second part to the miracle that we tend to miss. After Jesus gets the storm to stop raging, the wind to stop howling, and the waves to stop crashing, it became completely calm— immediately.

Think about this.

Even when a storm stops, the waves, the swells, take time to slow down.

But Jesus, the Creator and Sovereign Ruler of the universe, commands the storm to cease completely.

And it does.

The disciples had seen Jesus do one miracle after another. They, of all people, should have known He could handle this situation, too. There was no need to be afraid.

But we do the same thing. God has brought us through one storm after another, and then another one hits, and we completely forget His faithfulness.

If you're going to make it through the storms in life, you need to remember that God is with you, God cares about what you're going through, and God is in control.

We often don't understand the storms, and there's a lot that we won't understand until we get to heaven. But nothing is beyond God's control.

Fear comes into play when we experience things in life that are beyond our own control, and the reality is, there's a lot that we have no power, authority, or control over, and that can cause a lot of fear and uncertainty.

But each of those situations, those proverbial storms, are an opportunity for us to exercise and grow in our faith.

I love the way the prophet Jeremiah expresses faith in 32:17: "Sovereign Lord, You have made the heavens and the earth by Your great power and outstretched arm. Nothing is too hard for You" (NIV).

Now, notice this.

Before they got into the boat, Jesus said to His disciples, "Let us go over to the other side" (Mark 4:35 NIV).

The very fact that He said they were going to the other side means it was inevitable that they were going to *get* to the other side.

Now, He didn't say it would be an easy trip. He didn't say they wouldn't get cold and wet, that they wouldn't be frightened, or that it would be smooth sailing. He simply said, "Let us go over to the other side" (Mark 4:35 NIV).

And if He said it, they were going to make it.

In seasons of fear and uncertainty, of trials and storms, we can be confident in the outcome, of the "other side," because of who God is.

Notice that Jesus said to the disciples: "Why are you afraid? Do you still have no faith?" (Mark 4:40 NLT).

Jesus told the disciples two things: The root of their problem was *fear*.

The solution to their problem was faith.

You see, the greatest threat to the lives of the disciples was not the storm. It was their lack of faith.

It's interesting to me that you never see an instance in the Bible where Jesus rebukes someone for having too much faith.

Can you believe in God too much? Can you have too much faith?

You never see that.

I think God is pleased when we reach our limit, because in that moment, it's beyond us. And it's the perfect opportunity for Him to demonstrate His power, His character, and His love for us.

The problem was always a lack of faith. It's easy to live a "Christian" life that doesn't require any faith. And those lives are probably comfortable and safe. But scripture is definitive on the point: "Without faith, it is impossible to please God" (Hebrews 11:6 NIV).

If God knew in advance that the storm was going to be out there, why did He let them go through it? Why didn't He just wait for the storm to pass?

Because He wanted them to learn a lesson that can only be learned by experience. We never learn this lesson from a preacher or a Bible study or a podcast or a book.

Jesus can be trusted in the storms of life.

It's when we respond to the storms in life with faith that we see God's power most visibly—because He is the only One who can calm storms, literal and proverbial—and we sense His presence most intensely.

Storms are inevitable. They're going to come.

Storms are unpredictable. When they come, they come without warning.

Storms are impartial. It doesn't matter who you are or how well or how poorly you live, storms are a universal experience.

And they are also temporary. They don't last.

Situational, relational, emotional. They all run out of rain, and God's Word assures us that we are called to keep on living and to do so without fear. The sun will shine again, and hope will pour through because God is overwhelmingly faithful to be with us, always. And Jesus has already said we're going to the other side.

CHAPTER 3 STUDY QUESTIONS

Question: We talked about the different kinds of storms—situational, relational, and emotional— that we're likely to experience on this side of heaven. Have you experienced any of these storms? If so, which one(s)? What was the experience like? How did those storms make you feel?

_____
_____
_____
_____
_____
_____

Question: Consider the storm(s) you recalled in the first question. How did you react? After reading the chapter, how can you respond to future storms? What can equip you to respond in faith over fear?

_____
_____
_____
_____
_____
_____

Journal: The Bible teaches us that we have agency in our lives—that is, we have the freedom to choose. This is especially important when we're facing difficulties that seem as if they're never going to let up. How can you use faith to choose how you respond to storms?

_____

_____

_____

_____

_____

_____

Action: Storms in life are inevitable and unavoidable, but it doesn't mean that we can't be prepared to weather them. God's word equips us with the encouragement and strength we need to walk through storms in faith, rather than in fear. Identify some key verses to write down and keep handy when a storm crops up in your life.

_____

_____

_____

_____

_____

_____

CHAPTER 4
A BOUT WITH THE VIRUS OF DOUBT

I WANT TO TALK TO YOU ABOUT SOMETHING THAT YOU OR SOMEONE in your oikos (your relational network—the people God has supernaturally and strategically placed in your life) may be dealing with during this season of life.

Doubt.

How do we deal with and overcome the virus of doubt?

Sometimes, the culture of Christianity doesn't leave room for doubts.

Friends, please hear me.

If you or someone you know is wrestling with doubt in this season, you are not alone.

Even the disciples, the men who were with Jesus every day for three years, witnessing and participating in His ministry, still experienced doubts—even as He was bound for the cross. In fact, I'd argue that their doubts were probably the most pronounced in the days leading up to Good Friday.

They doubted that He was who he said he was. They doubted His goodness. They doubted His presence. They doubted His Lordship.

Suffice to say, the disciples had some serious doubts about their Teacher. Yet, keep in mind, Jesus used them mightily. Even Peter, the biggest doubter of them all, received a calling from Jesus who called him the rock upon which He would build His church (Matthew 16:18 NLT).

And Peter wasn't alone with his doubts.

I want to take a moment to pause and clarify that doubt isn't necessarily a bad thing. We have a tendency as Christians to beat ourselves up in those moments of doubt. But the truth is, we all wrestle with doubt to some degree.

In my work as a pastor, I encounter people—God-fearing men and women—who come to me, terrified that their salvation is somehow compromised by their questions and hesitations. In a word: terrified of their doubts.

A while back I received a note from a member of the congregation:

Dear Pastor Jeremy, I need your help. I wish I didn't have doubts. But I feel like I've got more questions than answers. And now I'm beginning to doubt whether I'm a Christian at all. Can you relate to any of that? What should I do?

Letters and emails like this don't bother me because they're honest and real, and I'm glad they are reaching out.

Can you relate?

Can you help me?

Here's someone who was refusing to hide their skepticism and pretend everything was OK when it really wasn't. And as a pastor and fellow believer, I'm so proud of the courage and vulnerability it takes to do that. Because I know it isn't easy to express your doubts and hesitations and questions. In fact, there have been some seasons in my life where I've faced doubts and been challenged to wrestle with them.

And if you're reading this, my guess is that you have too.

Sometimes our doubts stem from an issue that we're having that's persistent and loud. And maybe we've prayed about it, surrendered it to God, searched for answers, hoped for discernment and wisdom and relief. And instead of receiving an answer, maybe we've come up against silence, and so those prayers feel as though they've fallen on deaf ears.

Sometimes we pray, and it seems like God isn't listening.

Let's take a recent, real-world example. In 2020, COVID-19 became a global pandemic in a matter of weeks.[1] We encountered an unpredictable, highly contagious virus that has a wide array of effects on the human body. And amid the fear and uncertainty, we, as Christians, prayed for an end—a cure, the return of health to our nation and world. And God's response sometimes takes longer than we want.

It's easy for doubts to creep in alongside impatience.

I think, for us to continue, it would be helpful to discuss some basic misconceptions about the concept of doubt as it relates to Christianity.

But first, I want to share something with you.

Do you want to know why I'm doing what I'm doing now? Do you want to know why I'm pastoring today?

I'm a pastor today because I had doubts and questions. And I started investigating. That investigation led me to Bible college and my first degree in biblical studies with an emphasis in exposition, also known as the practice of taking the Bible apart and understanding what it really means.

And I learned and grew hungrier.

So, I went after my master's degree and then wanted more, so I went for a second one, learning and growing and digging in and getting answers for my questions and doubts; then went back and got my doctorate because I wanted to learn more. I did all this while serving in full-time ministry. I needed the confidence to know:

that Jesus Christ is who the Bible says He is;

that my doubts and questions would be answered,

and that I knew exactly what it was and who it was that I was committing my life to.

Now, I'm not saying that you should run out and get your MA, MDIV, or PhD in biblical studies. But I want to encourage you to seek answers amid your doubts because it is far too easy to let those doubts linger.

Go after it.

Get your questions answered. Research your doubts.

When I went looking, I found truth after truth after truth.

But to seek truth, we need to understand the nature of doubt.

And doubt can be good.

This seems counterintuitive, I know. Hang tight.

ALL ABOUT DOUBT

Doubt, as I've experienced it, can be a good thing if it leads you to discover more of the truth. But there's a caveat to this: Too many people leave their doubts lingering without getting after the answers to their questions. When we allow doubt to linger unaddressed like this, it can have a negative impact on our beliefs and our relationship with God. And lingering, unaddressed doubt can keep us from living in faith over fear.

A perfect New Testament example embodies this tendency and its impact.

I have a question for you. How would you like to be remembered for your biggest mistake?

Did you know that before he was "doubting Thomas," his family, friends, and neighbors used to call him Thomas the Titan? Big, strong guy expresses some serious doubts and ends up remembered for all of history not as a titan, but as a doubter.

OK, so I made up the titan thing, but you get the idea. Onto our story.

Thomas was one of the twelve disciples. He'd been hanging out with Jesus, and suddenly they're walking out the week leading up to Passover, known more commonly to us as Easter. But this was a holy week for the Jews, who would've been journeying to Jerusalem to observe the Passover seder meal in observance of their deliverance from Egypt.

So, weight and reverence was certainly owed to this week, but

Jesus's disciples still seem woefully unprepared for the events about to take place.

For instance, Jesus fulfills Old Testament prophecy in coming to earth as God incarnate born of a virgin (Isaiah 7:14; Luke 1:35 NLT) in Bethlehem (Micah 5:2; Matthew 2:4–6 NLT) who preached righteousness to the Jews (Psalm 40:9; Matthew 4:17 NLT) and taught in parables to the crowds (Psalm 78:1–2; Matthew 13:34–35 NLT)—who, on the whole, refused to listen (Isaiah 6:9–10; Matthew 13:13–15 NLT). This Redeemer (Isaiah 42:1–4; Matthew 12:15–21 NLT) who was hated by the people He came to serve (Isaiah 53:3; Luke 4:28–29 NLT), rode into Jerusalem during Holy Week on a donkey (Zechariah 9:9; Matthew 21:8–10 NLT) and was betrayed in exchange for thirty pieces of silver by one of the men who had walked with him for three years (Zechariah 11:12–13; Matthew 27:6–10 NLT).

And less than a week after his beloved teacher rides triumphantly into Jerusalem, the people who had laid palm leaves at His feet turn Him over to the religious leaders, and they mock, beat, and crucify Him.

And Thomas, witnessing these things, is taken aback, having expected none of these things to come to pass, despite Jesus's miracles and proclamations throughout His ministry. Thomas's whole world has been turned upside down, and suddenly all these doubts—past and present—are lingering.

In John's gospel account, he recounts:

> One of the twelve disciples, Thomas ...was not with the others when Jesus came. They told him, "We have seen the Lord!" But he replied, "I won't believe it unless I see the nail wounds in his hands, put my fingers into them, and place my hand into the wound in his side." (John 20:24–25 NLT)

This guy needs evidence.

And he gets it eight days later when all the disciples, including Thomas, were together (John 20:26a NLT).

"The doors were locked; but suddenly, as before, Jesus was standing among them" (John 20:26b NLT).

Boom. Out of nowhere.

And He opens with, "Peace be with you" (John 20:26c NLT)

Let's just pause a moment and put ourselves in the room with Thomas, the disciples, and Jesus.

They're hanging out, having fellowship, and suddenly there's a person in the room. And not just any person, but the person they had walked and talked and prayed and healed and broken bread with for three years. The person who they had watched suffer and die. And he appears supernaturally. No warning—no fireworks or loud noises to precede Jesus's appearance. He's simply there.

This is more than enough to rock the disciples. These men who, if anyone, would know and believe in Jesus's divinity.

Can you imagine that scene? Mind-blowing.

Then Jesus says to Thomas, "Put your finger here, and look at my hands. Put your hand into the wound in my side. Don't be faithless any longer. Believe!" (John 20:27 NLT).

How great is that? Thomas gets to have his evidence right in front of him. He's seeing it, touching it, hearing it. The tangibility of Jesus's appearance puts all his doubts to rest.

"'My Lord and my God!' Thomas exclaimed.

Then Jesus told him, 'You believe because you have seen me. Blessed are those who believe without seeing me.'" (John 20:28–29 NLT)

That bit at the end there? That's for us. That's for all of us down through the ages.

Because naturally we'd like to see Jesus appear, embodied.

Some of us might be inclined to reach out and touch his nail-scarred hands, the wound in his side.

For some of us, that might be enough for us to believe.

But Jesus didn't do that.

Because He wants us to have faith. And faith is believing without seeing.

"My Lord and my God."

Even Thomas's exclamation of belief was not enough to erase the impact of his doubt. No, for all of history, he's remembered as the disciple who doubted, so he's stuck with the enigma, Doubting Thomas.

What if you were remembered for your greatest mistake? What would your name be? Think about that for a second.

But here's the point: Despite his enigma, Thomas's doubt drove him to the truth. He professed and proclaimed Jesus Christ the moment his doubt was answered.

And this is important. Doubt can become dangerous if it's left unchecked.

Doubt can drive you to the truth.

Thomas's faith was driven so deep into his soul by having personally checked out the evidence of the resurrection that he spent the rest of his life declaring that it was true, that Jesus was the one and only Son of God.

Had his doubts been left unchecked, unaddressed, and unresolved, Thomas's faith could have wavered and burned out. And the same is true for us. But when we investigate and challenge and seek the truth to answer those questions, we can have a vibrant, life-giving faith.

In fact, despite popular belief, and if this story teaches us anything, it's that doubt and faith can coexist.

We seem to have a cultural misconception as Christians that places doubt and faith in opposition to one another.

Our natural inclination when we encounter or experience doubt is to beat ourselves up. Because if we were "good" Christians, we wouldn't have doubts, right? We feel terrible. We aren't supposed to doubt. Right?

Hear me, friends. Doubt is not the opposite of faith.

The opposite of faith is unbelief. And there's a big difference between unbelief and doubt. And that's an important distinction for us to make.

Unbelief is a willful refusal to believe. It's a deliberate decision to deny God. Period.

Doubt, on the other hand, is to be indecisive. I'm not sure about that. I sure hope this is right. I'm not certain, but I think so.

And that's OK.

Faith and doubt can coexist.

And to prove it, I have another story to tell you.

Jesus and a handful of his disciples are descending a mountain, and in their absence, a crowd has gathered around the other disciples, some Pharisees, and a man with his demon-possessed son.

What a picture.

This crowd, as Jesus, Peter, James, and John draw nearer, is arguing, and the father of the demon-possessed child brings his qualms to Jesus.

"Teacher, I brought my son so you could heal him. He is possessed by an evil spirit that won't let him talk. And whenever this spirit seizes him, it throws him violently to the ground. Then he foams at the mouth and grinds his teeth and becomes rigid. So I asked your disciples to cast out the evil spirit, but they couldn't do it" (Mark 9:17–18 NLT).

Can you imagine this father's heart in this moment?

It's obvious he's heard about this Jewish teacher who can perform miracles, and he's watched his son be controlled by an evil spirit, helpless to do anything about it. For this Middle Eastern father, Jesus is the shred of hope he can't bear to let go of.

When he arrives at the place where Jesus is rumored to be teaching and finds him absent, he turns, likely in a last-ditch kind of hope, to the disciples, to whom Jesus had given the ability to heal as well (Mark 6:7–13 NLT).

Can you imagine his distress, his hopelessness, when they are unable to heal his boy?

My guess is that when Jesus does show up, this father's heart is full of doubt where there was once faith. After all, his disciples had failed. The rumors were too good to be true. And what was he really expecting from this carpenter from Nazareth?

After hearing his plea and expressing His disappointment with the crowd, his disciples, and the father of the demon-possessed boy for their lack of faith, Jesus asks that the boy be brought to him and questions the father about how long he's been possessed. When he explains the situation to Jesus, he pleads, full of doubt but with a final shred of hope, "Have mercy on us and help us, if you can" (Mark 9:19–22 NLT).

I get the sense that Jesus's response to this heartbroken, grief-stricken father is meant not to chastise him for his doubts but is instead a challenge to believe in the face of those doubts.

"What do you mean, 'If I can'?" Jesus asked. "Anything is possible if a person believes" (Mark 9:23 NLT).

And the boy's father cries out:

"I do believe; but help me overcome my unbelief!" (Mark 9:24 NLT).

What a statement.

"Help me overcome my unbelief!"

This man was swimming in doubts, disappointments, and concerns. But he wasn't resigned to unbelief. Not yet.

And Jesus honored his profession of faith and cast out the demon from his son (Mark 9:25–27 NLT)—even amid the man's doubts.

But our story isn't over yet.

After Jesus heals the boy, his disciples draw him aside and ask why they couldn't cast out the demon themselves. And Jesus tells them that it was because that kind of demon could only be cast out by prayer (Mark 9:28–29 NLT).

It's easy to brush off a discussion like this. But sit with me in this for a minute.

The disciples were having issues with healing because they were trying to perform miracles in their own power and thinking that they could get by without prayer. And isn't it interesting? As a pastor, I'd say that's one of the biggest issues with the church today in having and embracing and experiencing the power that Jesus Christ offers to us. We lack prayer.

And when we have a lack of prayer, doubt is sure to follow.

"I do believe; but help me overcome my unbelief!"

You may have questions or concerns about some facet of the Christian faith. And that's OK. In fact, you can have a strong faith and still have some doubts. You can be a full-fledged Christian without having to feel like every single matter of faith and life has been 100 percent absolutely settled in your life.

Keep searching. Keep reading. Keep praying. Keep wrestling.

It's been said that struggling with God over the issues of life does not show a lack of faith. That *is* faith.

Here's the reality; even the strongest faith is going to have some mixture of doubt.

Pastor and theologian Timothy Keller said, "A faith without some doubts is like a human body without any antibodies in it. People who blithely go through life too busy or indifferent to ask hard questions about why they believe as they do will find themselves defenseless against either the experience of tragedy or the probing questions of a smart skeptic." [2]

DOUBTS CAN BE HELPFUL

If you want another biblical example, just read the Psalms, especially those of David.

When we look at David in the Psalms, we see a man who cries out to God often and with honesty. We see him asking questions of God that sometimes seem to betray a lack of faith.

God, where are You?

He's doubting God's presence. *God, why are you letting that happen?* He's doubting God's promises.

God, why is this happening to me?

He's doubting God's care.

We read him questioning where God is, if He'll be faithful to His promises, if God is capable, if God is good, and if God is just.

We go through the Psalms, and these questions resonate with us. And David is a man after God's own heart (1 Samuel 13:14 NKJV), even in his doubts.

And do you want to know why?

Because doubt is not unforgivable.

Some people have asked me in counseling if doubt is the unpardonable sin that the Bible talks about.

I have some good news for you if your head is swimming in doubts about God and His justice and sin and the resurrection and anything else you're wrestling with.

Doubt is not an unpardonable sin. In fact, it's not even a sin.

God doesn't condemn us when we have questions. A great biblical example of this is John the Baptist.

If anybody in history should have been sure about who Jesus is, it would have been John the Baptist. He's the guy who pointed at Jesus and said, "Behold the Lamb of God who takes away the sin of the world" (John 1:29 NLT).

Not only that, but he baptized Jesus. He was present when the spirit of God spoke from the heavens and said, "This is My beloved son, in whom I'm well pleased" (Matthew 3:17 NKJV). He saw the heavens open and heard the voice of God, and he should have been one who had no doubts.

Yet, he did.

This is so interesting to me.

He had incredible faith. But he ends up being arrested and jailed for denouncing the marriage of Herod Antipas with his sister-in-law, Herodias (Matthew 14:1–12; Mark 6:14–29 NLT). The tides turn, and he comes down with the virus of doubt.

Isn't that what happens to all of us when things don't go the way we think they should be going?

When expectations and reality fail to coincide in our lives, the virus of doubt has room to worm its way in.

That might be where you are today. Circumstances are tough, we're feeling cabin fever, we're getting impatient, and we're wondering.

This happens to John the Baptist.

He's not so sure. He's uncertain. He's questioning.

To resolve this, he sends two of his friends to go check Jesus out and ask Him, point blank:

"Are you the One to come, or should we be looking for someone else?" (Luke 7:19 NIV).

How does Jesus react?

What is wrong with John?

The idiot!

If anybody should know who I am, it's John!

Nope. He doesn't criticize him, doesn't slam him, and doesn't disqualify him from any role in the kingdom of God.

Instead, Jesus answers the two friends John sent, saying:

"Go back and report to John what you have seen and heard: The blind receive sight, the lame walk, those who have leprosy are cleansed, the deaf hear, the dead are raised, and the good news is proclaimed to the poor" (Luke 7:22 NIV).

This is the first recorded instance of a mic drop.

In other words, when we remember what Jesus has done in the past, it can help us with our doubts in the present.

John needed a reminder amid his isolation and confinement.

Let me ask you: How does John's expression of doubt affect Jesus's opinion of him?

After this episode, Jesus gets up and looks the people in the eye and says, "I tell you the truth, of all who have ever lived, none is greater than John the Baptist" (Matthew 11:11 NLT).

Think about the implications of this. John had doubted.

And Jesus paid John the highest compliment in the world in the very same moment that John has questions, concerns, and doubts.

When we have questions, concerns, and doubts, God does not slam us. In fact, He wants to talk with us—in those moments especially. Because we need to remember that we have a relational God. And in any relationship, there must be honesty.

So, doubt can be a good thing.

Doubt and faith can absolutely coexist. And doubt is not unforgivable.

One of the most useful antidotes to the virus of doubt that's available to us is to remember the evidence of God's presence in our own lives.

Remember the things you've seen and heard and experienced.

Even before I was a believer, I can recall times when God had his guiding hand on my life, where God's providence was in my life, where God was caring for me even though I hadn't acknowledged him at that point.

I can look back and see clearly now through people, circumstances, and places I had been and situations I found myself in that God was giving me evidence of his care, his providence, and his love for me even though I was a nonbeliever at the time.

And now, throughout many years of being a Christian, it's so clear how He has guided and directed my life.

If you're struggling with doubts and seeking answers and needing reminders of who God is, of where you've been, of what

He's brought you out of, of what He's guided you through, go back and remember those things in your own life.

Write it down.

Type it out.

Pray in thanks.

And watch your doubts work in you a stronger faith.

CHAPTER 4 STUDY QUESTIONS

Question: Often, doubt can be perceived as a negative thing, especially when we're talking about faith and the Bible. In what situations and areas of life do you experience doubt? How does this impact your faith? Your fears?

_____

_____

_____

_____

_____

_____

Question: Think about the different ways we can perceive doubt; it can be a negative experience that keeps us from belief, or it can be a positive experience that spurs deeper spiritual and relational growth. How do you conceptualize doubt? What can you do to shift your perspective on doubt?

_____

_____

_____

_____

_____

_____

Journal: John the Baptist is considered a person of tremendous faith. How does the account in Luke 7 regarding John's experience of doubt impact your understanding of John the Baptist? What does Jesus's response to John's doubt show us about the nature and purpose of doubt? Of faith?

_____

_____

_____

_____

_____

_____

Action: Identify a specific area of doubt. It can be a question you have, or a worldview you can't wrap your head around, or an issue that's heavy on your heart—anything that stirs up doubt for you. How can you restructure the way you think about that area of doubt? Does this change the way you interact with your doubts? By extension, how does it impact your faith?

_____

_____

_____

_____

_____

_____

CHAPTER 5
THE CURE

So, doubt is not the antithesis of faith; it's part of it.

But it's also not something to dwell on.

Because when we do, we start to live from a place of fear, not a place of faith.

So how do we overcome doubt?

I want to talk about how we treat it.

But just like with any kind of sickness or virus, we can't begin to treat the virus of doubt until we know its source. And once we know its source, we can better understand its nature. And once we know the nature of how it infects us, we can begin to cultivate a cure that works.

HOW DOUBT CAN INFECT US

There are at least three ways that doubt can begin to take root and negatively impact our spiritual well-being.

If we're considering the origins of the virus of doubt, we can confidently claim that doubt often begins in the mind. It can infect our intellect particularly effectively if we don't know what we really believe. Doubts commonly arise from misunderstandings we have about who God is, how He has revealed himself, and how He operates.

You may know a lot about the love and the forgiveness and the mercy of God. But if you don't know anything about the righteousness and the holiness and the justice and the fear of God, then you're going to wonder why He doesn't do certain things that you think He ought to do, and, conversely, why He does things that you think He shouldn't do.

You see, when our understanding of God is limited to the most appealing aspects of His character but ignores the full truth of who He is—truth that can be challenging to accept sometimes—doubt begins to take root in those gaps in our understanding. In fact, doubt thrives in our minds when we don't have a fully formed picture of who God is.

But the problem isn't with God—it's with our understanding of who He is.

If our understanding is restricted to God's goodness, love, grace, and mercy—all incredible, praiseworthy things—but fails to account for His justice, righteousness, and holiness, then we may fall into the trap of believing that God has promised to answer all our prayers in the way that we want them to be answered. And when we pray and our prayers aren't answered the way we expect them to be, we begin to doubt that He's there at all.

Some people think that God promises health and wealth to everybody who follows Jesus Christ. And when they're not particularly healthy and not particularly wealthy, then they begin to doubt His character and His presence.

And friends, the problem isn't with God.

He never promised us those things, though He certainly does do those things from time to time. The problem is with us in having an inaccurate view of who He is that allows questions and uncertainties and doubts to take root and dwell in our minds.

And the rooted indwelling of doubt has the dangerous potential to grow through emotions.

This can happen in several ways.

One of the most prominent ways in which doubt grows through emotions is when you have a faith that is fundamentally based on feelings. When the euphoria of a come-to-Jesus moment becomes the foundation of a relationship with Christ, it creates the perfect conditions for doubt to grow and expand.

I want to clarify that I'm not downplaying the emotional connection and experience that's possible (and even likely to happen) when you accept Christ. I had a very real experience when I accepted Christ. The weight that was lifted was real. It can be an exhilarating experience to know that all your sins are forgiven and that you're going to spend eternity in heaven.

But with some people, it's an emotional high that isn't substantiated and doesn't last. That euphoria begins to taper off, and when it does, people begin to think that their faith is going away. The feeling isn't the same, so they think there's a problem with their faith, and they begin doubting. I'm not getting goosebumps or (holy spirit bumps as some people say) or crying at every worship song or you fill-in-the- blank anymore.

In reality, they're misunderstanding the relationship between feelings and faith.

Faith is not fundamentally about feelings and emotions. Faith is fundamentally a decision of the will to follow Jesus Christ.

Let me ask you something.

What's fear?

How would we describe it? As a feeling, right?

Feelings can absolutely be a blessing, but they can't be the thing we let our faith rely on. And we're called to live in faith over fear.

Fear is a feeling that shifts and changes, and it is unreliable.

Faith is a choice that we make and that God sustains.

Our faith doesn't ebb and flow according to how emotionally charged up we are.

Another way doubts can enter our emotions is through emotional scarring that has taken place in our past.

For instance, you may have suffered abuse from a parent when you were a child. Your parents may have gone through a divorce, and you've never spoken to your dad again. Or maybe a spouse left you. And experiencing that kind of abandonment can often lead to chronic doubts toward God. You're just waiting for God to let you down.

Just like your dad. Or your mom. Or your spouse.

If you go through history and look at the lives of the most famous atheists who've ever lived—Karl Marx, Sigmund Freud, Bertrand Russell, Madelyn Murray O'Hare, Nietzsche, every Raiders fan who ever existed (just kidding … mostly)—you look at their lives, and every single one of them either had a father who died when they were young or who abandoned them when they were young, or they had a horrible, abusive relationship with their dad. Every single one.

Atheism and having a bad parent are not mutually exclusive concepts. And for most people, that kind of experience doesn't lead to atheism. But it does create barriers between those people and God.

Why?

Because they may have such deep-rooted anger toward their earthly fathers that it's hard—if not impossible—to even consider the possibility of a heavenly Father that they would even want to know.

Or individuals who have experienced emotional trauma may feel like if they put their trust in God, they're going to end up being abandoned, whether that person left them through death or divorce or whatever. And it's tempting to think, *"I'm not falling for that again."*

It's important to bear in mind that emotions can create barriers between us and God, whether we're aware of them or not.

And for as easily as doubt can grow in our minds and through our emotions, they can become entrenched in the will just as easily.

Doubt can come in through our point of decision.

We have opportunities to make decisions all the time. Right and wrong.

If you're a follower of Jesus Christ, and you have made the willful decision to continue to pursue a pattern of sinful and immoral behavior in your life—you've got this one area where you don't want to let God in—doubts will have every opportunity to grow.

Why?

Because sin introduces a lack of peace in our lives.

When you struggle for lack of peace you begin to wonder.

Where is God to give me peace I'd hoped to have as a Christian? What happened to, "my peace I leave with you?" (John 14:27 NIV).

Sin creates distance between us and God. When you're harboring a sinful pattern of behavior in your life, you don't want to bring yourself wholly into the presence of God because you're afraid you're going to be confronted with your sin. You kind of hang back, keep your distance, and God seems to be nowhere in sight.

Let me offer an illustration.

Imagine that you have a small cardboard box. And imagine that this little box contains some small hidden sin that you keep to yourself. And it's such a small box. No harm, no foul, right?

Wrong.

What this little box of your compartmentalized sin does is create distance between you and God. We also tend to think this box is so little that it's no big deal. But whatever it is, whatever secret sin we're keeping from God, it never stays this size. It may start small, but if left unconfessed, it soon grows and multiplies until there's not only distance but a barrier between you and God.

Our own decisions to follow our sin make us reluctant to fully engage with God. When we willfully follow our sinful desires and behaviors, we're engaging our own will—not God's—and that creates a barrier between us and God.

And amid this, you begin to feel that God's presence is distant or worse yet, gone. And you begin to doubt that He's there at all.

Friends, please understand.

We must remember that when we feel distant from God, He hasn't moved. We have.

How do we bridge that gap? Confess. Confess. Confess.

Confession knocks those barriers down like the walls of Jericho. Immediate and comprehensive.

Doubts can breed in our minds, our emotions, our wills. But the key thing is what do you do with it when you've got it. What's the antidote for our doubts?

HOW TO CURE DOUBT

I want to preface this by saying that this is not easy.

There's no quick fix.

But there are some solid biblical principles we can follow that help us build up our immunity to doubt.

Let's talk solutions.

First, it's important to find the root of your doubt.

You've got to diagnose the source of how doubt has entered your life before you know how you can deal with it.

We've talked about several different examples of how doubts can enter through your mind, your emotions, and your will. And maybe you can see how doubt is coming into your life.

But maybe not.

Maybe I didn't hit on the specific thing that's true for you. And if that's the case, you need to think about what's caused doubt to take root in your life. It could be anything from a movie to a friend to a teacher or professor or parent or a long-held bias or belief.

As you think about it, don't do it on a surface level. Go deep and ask the tough questions of yourself. I mentioned in the last chapter that doubt, for me, was the catalyst that drove me to the answers I wanted and needed to know.

Instead of letting your doubts derail your mind, heart, and faith, let them lead you closer to God.

Many people struggle intellectually and wonder if the Bible can be trusted and if Jesus ever existed.

But the reality is that underneath those questions, there's something deeper. People sometimes use questions as a smokescreen to keep God at arm's length and obscure the real issue, which, if they're honest with themselves, is their pride.

I want to rule over my own life. King of my home. Captain of my ship. Boss of my world.

It's such an easy mentality to fall into. So be honest as you analyze the source of your doubt. And remember that you're never in it alone.

When searching for a cure, an anecdote, to the virus of doubt, it's okay to ask for help.

Remember how we talked earlier about honesty being an important part of our relationship with God?

Be honest with God and others.

Don't be afraid to ask God or trusted Christian friends questions as you wrestle with your doubt.

Remember the story about the father who came to Jesus Christ to plea for help for his son? I love what this father said to Jesus: "I do believe, help me overcome my unbelief!" (Mark 9:24 NIV).

He had a believing heart, a faith-filled heart—even if it was permeated with doubt (see chapter 4). And when he asked earnestly, Jesus responded with healing.

I understand this can be a difficult thing to do, to come before the God of the universe who's seen all our sin and ask for Him to grow our faith and quell our fears and doubts. But it's not out of bounds for us when we're wrestling with questions and issues to go to God and ask him to strengthen our faith.

In James 2:4, Jesus's brother makes it clear: "We do not have because we do not ask" (NIV).

Friends, go to God, not as a last resort, but as your first priority. Ask God to lead you to wisdom in answer to your questions. Ask him to bring people into your life who can help you wrestle well with your doubts and grow in your faith.

And ask other Christians for help too. The Bible is so clear about our deep need to seek community and fellowship with fellow believers: "Are you hurting? Pray. Do you feel great? Sing. Are you sick? Call the church leaders together to pray and anoint you with oil in the name of the Master. Believing-prayer will heal you, and Jesus will put you on your feet. And if you've sinned, you'll be forgiven—healed inside and out" (James 5:13–15 MSG).

That, dear friends, is how we engage in the healing process. This is how we begin to live in faith over fear. And once we reach that point, after seeking wisdom from God and others in how to deal with it, we are called and encouraged to take action—tangible, actionable steps to find our answers and grow our faith. In fact, scripture admonishes us not to sit with doubts and let them linger and fester, but rather to act: "Now that you know these things, you are blessed if you do them" (John 13:17 NIV).

If doubt has gained a foothold through your mind, and you have vague, generalized questions and objections, I'd like to challenge you to dig deeper and figure out what your specific questions and objections are. Sit down, take out a piece of paper, and make a list.

If doubt has gained a foothold through your emotions, you don't want to go through life with some sort of pain from your past that is an impediment to fully experiencing the joy and adventure of knowing Jesus fully. You might seek out some help from a pastor or counselor or someone who could help you resolve these issues from your past so you can enjoy more fully the presence of God and not be riddled with doubts and uncertainties.

If it's a question of your will, ask yourself where and what you're holding back from God. If you only give God 90 percent of your heart, then you leave 10 percent of your heart open for the doubts to come in. That 10 percent is more than enough space for doubt to reside and fester and grow.

And you have a choice to make.

You can continue to pursue your own agenda and then deal with the kind of doubts and uncertainties that that agenda raises in your relationship with God.

And some Christians choose this path.

Or you can choose to abandon the sin and pursuit of personal pleasure and satisfaction in favor of chasing after God, desiring to fully know Him and experience Him as the greatest pleasure you could possibly encounter if you would choose to follow His way.

That, friends, is the way of a faith that is vibrant and rich and strong and full of adventure.

And when you encounter this faith in earnest, you will naturally desire to put it into practice.

James writes definitively on the subject, imploring Christians to not simply listen to scripture, but to walk it out (James 1:22–25 NLT). Faith needs to be exercised, not simply embodied.

If we want to be able to fight off doubt, we need to be in shape.

Think about it this way. If we're healthy, if we're strong, if we're feeding ourselves appropriately, then a minor infection is less likely to become a major infection because our immune system is built up.

When we exercise and feed our faith, it grows deeper, and when doubts come in, they don't take a foothold, and they don't grow and destroy our faith. And one of the best ways to do that is to read the Word every day.

According to the International Bible Society, 87 percent of Christians do not read the Bible on a regular basis.[1]

Let me ask you something. How can you grow in your faith if you're not accessing the word of God on a regular basis?

You can't.

It's like with any kind of sport, habit, or discipline. If you don't practice, you don't get better. And if you don't spend time in the Word of God on a regular basis, you create the conditions under which doubt can not only creep in but thrive.

This may be a challenging habit for some of us to create. But I'm here to tell you, you don't have to do it on your own.

Building an immunity to doubt is strengthened and supported by connecting with people of strong faith because faith can be just as contagious as doubt.

If you surround yourself and seek out community and fellowship and study with people who have a strong, vibrant, passionate, and deep faith, you'll learn from them.

And the opposite is true as well. If you surround yourself with people who are always doubting and filling your mind with falsities and untruths, you'll learn from them, too.

We were made for community. None of us are sufficient or strong enough to weather bouts with doubt on our own. Regardless of what season of life and faith you're walking through, you need the company and fellowship and accountability of strong believers in your life. Paul warned the early church in Corinth about the dangers of relying exclusively on their own strength: "If you think you are standing strong, be careful not to fall" (1 Corinthians 10:12 NLT).

This verse is a great warning against pride. We're influenced by the people we choose to be around the most. And that's why it's so vital that we live in community alongside strong believers.

Wherever you are as you're reading these pages, I want to encourage you in your doubts, your struggles, and your questions:

No matter where you are,

no matter how prominent your doubts,

no matter how numerous your questions,

you can trust that God desires to quell your doubts and answer your questions because He's after your heart. And if you asked Him,

He would encourage you to continue seeking because He's promised that you'll find Him. "If you seek God … you'll be able to find him if you're serious, looking for him with your whole heart and soul" (Deuteronomy 4:29 MSG).

CHAPTER 5 STUDY QUESTIONS

Question: What are some ways that doubt has infected your heart and mind? How do they impact your relationship with God? Do they contribute to your experience of fear?

_____

_____

_____

_____

_____

_____

Question: The Bible talks extensively about the ways that sin impacts our relationship with God, and the chapter illustrates this concept by describing a small box filled with our sin that steadily grows to create a barrier between God and us. What sin is creating distance between you and God?

_____

_____

_____

_____

_____

_____

Journal: We've talked a bit about how our understanding of God impacts both our faith and our doubts. Examine your conception and understanding of God's character. Who is He to you? What is He like? How do you relate to Him, talk to Him, and interact with Him? What aspects of God's character do you struggle with?

_____

_____

_____

_____

_____

_____

Action: Look at the journal question and what you wrote about your understanding of God. Then, think about some of the cures mentioned in chapter 5. What practices (i.e., finding the root of your doubt, Bible study, fellowship) are lacking in your faith life? Which one(s) do you think would be helpful in curing your doubts? Which one(s) would help you deepen your relationship with and understanding of God?

_____

_____

_____

_____

_____

_____

CHAPTER 6
MADE FOR MORE

Do you remember Doubting Thomas in chapter 4? Do you recall the events he had witnessed prior to Jesus appearing and offering His wounds so Thomas might see and feel and believe?

This is the space where our story picks up. In between Holy Week and Thomas's belief, in the hours between Jesus's death and resurrection.

John's gospel account[1] begins early on Sunday morning, three days after Jesus had been mercilessly beaten and crucified and buried in a borrowed tomb, on the day He had promised the impossible.

It's almost too much to hope for the men and women who had been walking alongside Him—some since the beginning of His radical, countercultural ministry—and their grief is palpable.

So much so, that Mary Magdalene—who had been healed of her demon possession and who had become a faithful follower of Jesus (Luke 8:1–3 NLT)—rises early on Sunday morning, having observed the Sabbath the day before, according to Jewish custom, and goes to the tomb. I can imagine her weeping, torn between a slow, grief-laden walk and a run that will get her to her Lord's resting place faster. You see, though she knows Jesus, loves Him deeply, what He's promised to do today just doesn't seem possible. Yet, she must know if what He said is true.

Can you imagine her reaction when she comes upon the open tomb?

The massive, guarded stone the religious leaders had placed in front of this burial cave had been rolled away, the guards nowhere to be seen.

Maybe, she thinks, and runs to find Simon Peter and the disciple Jesus loved (who, traditionally, is thought to be John). As she's running, I can't help but think that she's also trying to rationalize what she's seen, and when she reaches the disciples, she exclaims, "They have taken the Lord's body out of the tomb, and we don't know where they have put him!" (John 20:2 NLT).

They run for the tomb immediately, and when they arrive, hearts pounding, they find the tomb exactly as Mary had described it.

John, who had arrived first, stoops to look inside—but doesn't enter—and finds the grave clothes lying empty on the floor. Then Simon Peter appears and enters, observing the lack of decaying flesh, the empty linen wrappings, the head cloth folded on a stone slab.

And they realize.

Jesus is exactly who He said He is.

THE MOMENT WE'VE ALL BEEN WAITING FOR

Christianity hinges on that moment.

The moment when prophecy becomes reality.

The moment when forgiveness becomes final.

The moment when the teaching carpenter from Nazareth becomes the risen Lord.

The resurrection story is vital to the Christian faith.

That is, if the resurrection of Jesus Christ did not occur, we don't have Christianity or a basis for hope, faith, or justice.

But it did occur, and because of that, we can know that we were made for more than divisiveness and anger and hurt and disappointment and just getting by.

Think about it this way: God took the worst possible situation—the death of His Son—turned it around, used it for good, and changed the world. The resurrection changed history. It was the moment in which the ways we relate to God shifted dramatically and significantly.

When you write out the year, what point do you start at? At what point are you counting from? How many years from what?

Jesus.

It's the most important event in history. More than that, it's still changing and forming and molding and transforming individual lives like yours and mine every day.

Friends, God made you for more. More than the daily grind. More than barely getting by. More than a fear-filled, faith-starved life. And because of the resurrection, we can experience the lasting change that Jesus ushers in.

Now, if you're a longtime Christian, you know and understand the significance of this. We're able to experience this new life that Jesus gives us when we accept His free gift of atonement, of each and every one of our sins washed clean and pure so that we can enter his presence holy and blameless in His sight.[2]

And this is a tremendous gift, truly.

But Jesus didn't give us this gift to keep it to ourselves. Instead, we're supposed to help others receive this gift as well. Just like the loaves and fish in chapter 2, the gift just keeps multiplying, and Jesus calls us, as longtime Christians who love Him, to feed His sheep, His people.[3] The ones who are difficult.

The ones who are combative. The ones who are broken.

Scripture tells us, "If we were put on friendly terms with God by the sacrificial death of His Son ... just think how our lives will expand and deepen by means of His resurrection life" (Romans 5:10 MSG).

This is the greatest of gifts. And it's for all people.

Not just religious people.

Remember, religious people put Jesus on trial.

And religious people condemned Him to death.

All the radical talk about people having a relationship with God was too countercultural, too accessible.

They wanted rules, rituals, regulations. In a word: control.

But the resurrection of Jesus is not meant for the religious elite with their ritualistic rhythms and their high-minded ideals and their prideful hearts.

So, if you're not a particularly religious person, you have little or no religious background, you don't really feel that connected to God, you rarely go to church, congratulations.

The resurrection of Jesus is for you.

YOU'RE INVITED

Jesus Christ did not come for religious people who kept up appearances of piety and who questioned His nearness to the broken. He came for the sinners, the disconnected, the hurting, the broken, the rule-breakers, the criminals, the destitute, the nonreligious. The people who could acknowledge their need and desire for relationship. Because that's what He's after.

"I'm here inviting outsiders not insiders—an invitation to a changed life, changed inside and out" (Luke 5:32 MSG).

Resurrection is God's invitation to you to have a changed life. To live from a place of faith over fear.

What do you want to change about your life?

Now, some of you reading this may be content with where you are and believe you're a good person, and I have no doubt that that's probably true. You pay your taxes and walk your dog and love your kids and go to church and love your spouse. And that's great.

But can I let you in on something?

It's nothing compared to what you could be. You're only using a fraction of your God-given potential. Friends, I'm here to tell you, you were made for more. You have barely scratched the surface.

Note: Surface.

When I talk about the transforming work of the resurrection, I don't mean changing your haircut or the paint on your living room walls or the carrying case for your Bible.

Changing the external things about us is not what makes the difference.

The Pharisees and religious leaders of Jesus's day took great pains to appear pious and upright. They wore the right clothing, recited the right prayers, made the right sacrifices at the right times, said the right things—all according to the law. And they probably expected a commendation from Jesus. Because on the outside, they were perfect.

But on the inside?

"What sorrow awaits you teachers of religious law and you Pharisees. Hypocrites! For you are like whitewashed tombs—beautiful on the outside but filled on the inside with dead people's bones and all sorts of impurity." (Matthew 23:27 NLT)

Changing the external does not change you because you've got to work on the internal.

And that is resurrection work.

HOW JESUS'S RESURRECTION CHANGES US

There are a few ways to approach internal, resurrection change. And it begins by opening our minds to God's power.

If we're going to engage in God-centered and God-fueled change, we've got to change the way we think. This can be a daunting task, but God never asks us to do the legwork alone. "Let God transform you into a new person by changing the way you think" (Romans 12:2 NLT).

We don't change by trying harder on the outside.

The average New Year's resolution lasts two weeks.[4] That's about how long willpower works. We change our lives by changing the way that we think and by opening our minds to the possibility of God—that He exists and that He loves us.

Barriers to change haven't changed as dramatically from biblical times as we may think. In Ephesians 4:18, Paul observes, "Many are far away from the life of God because they have shut their minds against Him. They can't understand His ways" (LB).

The reason we may not understand God is because we've closed our minds to Him, and until we open our minds to the possibility of God, there's not going to be any lasting change in our lives. And this can make it feel like any change is impossible.

From a human perspective, we sometimes desire change but fall short because we're limited in our abilities. We try and end up back at the start, and the constant striving in our own power and failing in our own power can be incredibly disheartening.

But if we look at it from God's perspective, we realize that God has power that we don't have.

God is not finite, limited, or restricted, and when we open our minds to the power of God, He can work incredible changes in our lives that we never thought possible.

Paul writes in Ephesians 1:19–20: "I pray that you'll begin to understand how incredibly great God's power is to help those who believe Him. It's the same mighty power that raised Christ from the dead" (LB).

Did you hear that?

The same power that raised Jesus Christ back to life two thousand years ago is the same power available to us to make changes in our lives.

If God has the power to raise the dead, He can raise a dead marriage.

He can raise a dead career. He can raise a dead dream.

God can do anything. But there's an important caveat to this: Understand.

Paul says, "I pray you'll *understand* how great His power is."

Living the "more" we were created for starts with opening our minds to the power of God. It starts with changing the patterns and postures of our minds. Because we were made for more than self-deprecation, and cynicism, and anger, and bitterness, and frustration.

And once we open our minds, we have room to soften our hearts to God's grace.

What is grace?

Grace is such a multifaceted term. At its core, grace is when God gives us what we need instead of what we deserve. Grace is also the power God gives us to enact the changes we need in our lives that we simply can't manage on our own. We all need grace, and we need to soften our hearts to receive it.

In today's environment of stress, anger, and division, we don't normally experience grace from other people. But God shows us grace 24/7. In fact, the next breath you're going to take is because God's grace gives it to you. Everything you and I have in life is a gift from God.

Some people get defensive about this and claim they earned what they have. They're hardworking, resourceful people. And while those things may be true, where do you think you got the power to earn it? Where do you think you got your brains, your health, your mind?

Hear me when I say that every thing and ability you have is because God is good and gives you what you need—not what you deserve. And that, friends, is grace. "God has showered upon us the richness of His grace for He understands us and knows what is best for us at all times" (Ephesians 1:8 LB).

Notice: At *all* times. Not some of the time. *All* the time.

God understands you better than you understand yourself. He's watched every moment of your life. He knows every thought you've ever had— good, bad, and ugly. He's seen it all, and He still loves you unconditionally.

That's called grace.

Sometimes we think we must help God's grace.

My friend recently bought his wife a yearlong house cleaning service for her birthday to help her out and lessen her load a little bit.

They both ended up hating it. Why?

Because every Thursday morning, they feel like they must get up early to "pick up" the house before the maids come.

Tell me, where's the logic in this? This guy is paying for people to come and clean his house, and he and his wife feel the need to clean it up first because they don't want anyone to think they're slovenly—even when cleaning is the literal service that group of people has been hired to perform.

Seems silly, doesn't it?

But a lot of people do that with God. We think we must get our lives cleaned up before we open up to God.

Listen friends.

He already knows all of it. Every inch of your body, every facet of your personality, every thought in your head, every mark on your character, every doubt, fear, worry, sin, every joy, triumph, victory, and dream.

And instead of leaving us to muddle through this life on our own, we can simply bring Jesus the good.

The bad. The ugly.

The embarrassing.

The stuff we are ashamed of.

The things nobody else knows about.

Bring all of it to Jesus, and He promises to give you the grace you need. Romans 3:22 puts it like this:

> God says He will accept us, acquit us, declare us not guilty for all the things we've done wrong in life if we trust Jesus Christ to take away our sins and we can all be saved in this same way by coming to Christ, no matter who we are or what we've been like" (LB).

Aren't you grateful for that last phrase?

No matter who we are or what we've been like, God says we can have His grace (2 Corinthians 12:9).

There's not a person in life who bats 1,000. We've all blown it. We've all made mistakes. But God wipes them out. And that's called grace.

When I was in elementary school, I hopped around a bit from school to school after my parents got divorced, and halfway through one school year, I was the new kid at W.D. Hall Elementary School in El Cajon, California.

The first day I was in there, the class was doing a volcano project, complete with an actual eruption with lava. And being the new kid, I was on my own; everybody else already had partners because they had friends. So, I set to work on my own.

My project was a disaster. I was so embarrassed. The thing was a mangled mess of goop. It was pathetic. I was so discouraged because I had really tried hard to make the thing work. I had wanted to impress my teacher and my new classmates, and instead, my project was a massive mess.

Have you ever felt that way about your life? You really try hard, and the thing you're trying hard to do well still isn't turning out right?

In the middle of this volcanic mess, my teacher walked over, looked at me, and said, "It's OK, son. You can start over, and this time I'll help you."

That's grace.

He didn't put me down.

He didn't call my project a disaster.

He simply said, "You can start over, and this time I'll help you."

And God says the same thing to us even after He's seen all that's gone on in our lives, all the messes we've made, all the times we've tried and failed, and He always gives us the opportunity to start over with His help. He always makes a way for us to walk in the way of faith over the way of fear (2 Corinthians 12:9, paraphrase).

And that's the difference. That's why it will turn out better than ever. So how do we engage with God's grace?

"Saving is all His idea, and all His work. All we do is trust Him enough to let him do it. It is God's gift from start to finish" (Ephesians 2:8 MSG).

This means we don't try harder. It means we trust Him enough to let Him do the work.

We will never earn God's grace because we will never deserve God's grace.

It's simply a gift, and all we do is humbly accept it.

"God gives grace to the humble. So, say a quiet yes to God, and He will be there in no time" (James 4:6–8 MSG).

I hope you'll do that today. I hope you'll say a quiet yes to God. I hope you'll open your mind, soften your heart, and receive his grace.

If you do that, you will never be the same again. You will see changes in your life that you never thought possible.

If you do that, it will make an incredible difference because God's grace changes everything. You will start to realize that you were made for more.

And when we accept and live in that grace, we're able to live our lives in and with God's love.

No one will ever love you more than God does. He loves you unconditionally; it's not based on anything you do. He loves you because He made you, and He created you so He could love you. And He created you to know and love Him back.

And Jesus's resurrection proves how much God loves you by His coming and dying on the cross—even before you knew it or understood it.

Paul writes to the early believers in Ephesus, imploring them to embrace this truth: "I pray that Christ will live in you as you open the door and invite Him in and that you will be able to feel and understand how long and wide and deep and high His love really is and to experience this love for yourselves" (Ephesians 3:16–19 MSG).

To feel and experience God is vital. And that is my prayer for you. That you will not just know in your mind that God's love for you exists, but that you will experience the love of God, and that from that experience would come transformation. Because it's only when you experience and feel the love of God that the transformative, internal, resurrection change begins.

THERE'S GRACE FOR THE PRODIGAL

If you think you're too far from grace and love, just read the story of the prodigal son in Luke 15:11–32 and you'll never doubt again.

The story of the prodigal is, in so many ways, our story, and friends, it is a picture of the unconditional love that God has for you.

It doesn't matter where you've been or what you've done. When you come home to God and say, "God, I've been disconnected from You. I've been going my own way. But I'm coming home," God throws a party for you and welcomes you back into His arms of love.

Luke's gospel puts it this way: "Count on it—there's more joy in heaven over one sinner's rescued life than over ninety-nine good people in no need of rescue" (Luke 15:7 MSG).

Therefore, the resurrection matters. This is why Jesus Christ went through the pain and suffering of Friday:

So that we could experience Sunday.

So that we could know that we were made for more.

So that we could live for more.

When you live your life in and with God's love, it absolutely changes everything.

> We throw open our doors to God and discover at
> the same moment that He has already thrown open
> His door to us!" (Romans 5:2 MSG)

You were made by God and for God, and until you understand that, life does not make sense.

We need to remember living with faith over fear is a realization of who God is and how He feels about us.

The Bible says: "There is no fear in love. But perfect love drives out fear" (1 John 4:18 NIV).

God's perfect love will drive out your fear so you can live in faith.

You were made for an eternal relationship with God, one that goes on long past this life. I hope you will do what Paul encourages believers to do in Romans 5:2 and "Throw open the doors of your life to God and say, 'Yes God, I'm coming home'" (MSG), because "Jesus has His arms wide open for you" (1 Corinthians 16:23 MSG).

So, dear friends, come home.

CHAPTER 6 STUDY QUESTIONS

Question: Most people are familiar with the Jesus story and the resurrection, whether they believe it was true or not. How do you make sense of the events in John 20:1–10? What does the resurrection mean to you? Who is Jesus to you?

_____

_____

_____

_____

_____

_____

Question: The resurrection of Jesus was a game-changer, and not just for life on the other side of heaven. The resurrection has real, right here, right now implications for our lives as followers of Jesus. What areas of your life are impacted by the resurrection? Do you feel like you're living out your God-given potential? Who do you believe God has created you to be?

_____

_____

_____

_____

_____

_____

Journal: Take a moment to reflect on the story of the prodigal child returning home, broken, to their parent after doing life in their own way. Have you ever experienced a moment like this? How did your family or friends respond? In what ways does your experience and that of the prodigal son and daughter change the way you understand who God is? Does this have an impact on your day-to-day life?

_____

_____

_____

_____

_____

_____

Action: Read John 20. How does the historical context impact your understanding of Jesus's resurrection? Your faith? Fears? Doubts? In what ways does this passage equip you and encourage you to walk in faith over fear?

_____

_____

_____

_____

_____

_____

CONCLUSION

I want to revisit that definition in Hebrews for a second. The one that tells us what faith is. The Message translation puts it this way:

> The fundamental fact of existence is that this trust in God, this faith, is the firm foundation under everything that makes life worth living. It's our handle on what we can't see. The act of faith is what distinguished our ancestors, set them above the crowd. (Hebrews 11:1 MSG)

Even in doubts.

Even in storms. Even in fear.

Faith, friends, is essential. It's fundamental to who we are and how we have relationship with God. And notice what isn't mentioned anywhere in this passage. Fear.

Do you want to know why everything changes, why we can handle those situations that seem impossible, why faith is so important to our walk with God?

Because we were made for so much more than struggling and striving.

We were made to walk in faith and trust and relationship with the Creator whose breath fills our lungs and who has proven Himself faithful to us time and time again and who is the very essence of Love itself. And perfect love, this Love that God is and that He offers to us casts out fear.[1]

And so, friends, we don't have to live from a place of fear amid the toughest, most doubt-filled storms that we'll encounter in this life. Instead, we can walk in faith, knowing we are deeply loved and deeply known by Love Himself.

May we live for more because we were made for more.

---

[1] 1 John 4:18

NOTES

INTRODUCTION

1   *Merriam-Webster, s.v.* "fear," accessed March 6, 2021, https:// www. merriam-webster.com/dictionary/fear.

CHAPTER 1: WALKING IN FAITH OVER FEAR

1   American Social History Project, "'Only Thing We Have to Fear is Fear Itself': FDR's First Inaugural Address," History Matters: The U.S. Survey Course on the Web, George Mason University, March 22, 2018, http:// historymatters.gmu.edu/d/5057/.
2   Blue Letter Bible, "Lexicon: Strong's H398 - *'ākal*," Blue Letter Bible, BLB Institute, accessed March 20, 2021, https: //www.blueletterbible. org/lang/lexicon/lexicon.cfm? t=kjv&strongs=h398.
3   Marc Bennetts, "Soviet Space Propaganda Was Atheistic — But Putin's Cosmonauts Fear God," *Insider,* July 24, 2014, https:// www.businessinsider. com/strange-connection-between-russian- astronauts-and-god-2014-7.
4   Julie Zauzmer, "In Space, John Glenn Saw the Face of God: 'It Just Strengthens My Faith,'" *Salt Lake Tribune,* December 11, 2016, https:// archive.sltrib.com/article.php?id=4699760&itype=CMSID.

CHAPTER 3: JESUS CALMS THE STORM

1   I encountered this information from a guide during my travels in Israel while on the Sea of Galilee.

2   Elizabeth Segran, "The $70 Billion Quest for a Good Night's Sleep," *Fast Company*, April 30, 2019, https://www.fastcompany.com/90340280/the-70-billion-quest-for-a-good-nights-sleep.

CHAPTER 4: A BOUT WITH THE VIRUS OF DOUBT

1   World Health Organization, "Archived: WHO Timeline — COVID-19," *WHO*, April 7, 2020, https://www.who.int/news/item/27-04-2020-who-timeline---covid-19.

2   Alisa Childers, "I Never Expected to Doubt," The Gospel Coalition, March 6, 2019, https:// www.thegospelcoalition.org/article/i-never-expected-doubt/.

CHAPTER 5: THE CURE

1   American Bible Society, *State of the Bible 2019*. Ventura: Barna, 2019, https://www.americanbible.org/uploads/ content/state- of- the-bible-2019_report_041619_final.pdf.

CHAPTER 6: MADE FOR MORE

1   John 20:1–10. For the purposes of this chapter, I've included a paraphrase of only the first ten verses, but I would encourage you to read the whole chapter to gain a fuller picture of the events surrounding the resurrection.

2   "Yet now he has reconciled you to himself through the death of Christ in his physical body. As a result, he has brought you into his own presence, and you are holy and blameless as you stand before him without a single fault" (Colossians 1:22 NLT).

3   "A third time he asked him, 'Simon son of John, do you love me?' Peter was hurt that Jesus asked the question a third time. He said, 'Lord, you

know everything. You know that I love you." Jesus said, 'Then feed my sheep'" (John 21:17 NLT).

4   Best Life Editors, "How Long Do New Year's Resolutions Last? This Is When Most People Quit," *Best Life*, December 30, 2019, https://bestlifeonline.com/new-years-resolutions-ditch-date/.

Printed in the USA
CPSIA information can be obtained
at www.ICGtesting.com
LVHW041142171023
761327LV00039B/385

9 781664 274235